SEO
MADE
SIMPLE®

2020

Insider Secrets For Driving More Traffic To Your Website - Instantly

7th Edition

by
Michael H. Fleischner

SEO Made Simple®
2020

(Seventh Edition)

Search Engine Optimization
Copyright © 2020 by Michael H. Fleischner

ISBN: 9798607258344

Library of Congress Cataloging in Publication Data is on file with the publisher

Printed in the United States of America

To Jamie, Samantha and Alex-
My inspiration and joy

To my father, brother, and extended family

In memory of my mother

Contents

BONUS: See page 135 for access to a special download!

SEO Made Simple
7th Edition

Foreword

It's amazing how the art and science of search engine optimization (SEO) continues to evolve, and this past year was no exception. In addition to the ever present Google updates, social influence, and artificial intelligence, Google is continually expanding search. The goal of this book is to make the idea of top rankings simple for you. SEO can be complex but the core philosophy of *SEO Made Simple*® has not changed, it has simply evolved. What you'll find in this 7th edition is more than just tactical updates on search engine optimization; you'll find a shift away from some of the more traditional aspects of SEO towards factors influencing rankings today: engaging content, mobile search, local search, online reviews, social media, and more. In my opinion, this evolution affecting search engine optimization doesn't have to make it more complex. In fact, it simply reinforces what Google has been talking about all along, improving the user experience for those seeking information online.

According to Internet Live Stats, Google now processes over 40,000 search queries every second on average, which translates to over 3.5 billion searches per day and 1.2 trillion searches per year worldwide. Add the number of interactions with social media and mobile apps, and ranking well on Google search can become overwhelming. The good news is that search engines are still the dominant resource for finding and cultivating information on the web, so focusing your efforts on organic search can pay huge dividends for websites and blogs.

Whether you're new to SEO or simply looking for the most effective strategies to dominate Google, having an understanding of basic search engine optimization techniques, supplemented with knowledge of the latest algorithm changes, puts you ahead of 95% of those trying to "optimize" their website. I've updated this guide to include the latest information, tools, and resources you can begin using immediately to command top organic placements for your website, blog, apps, and other digital assets. I have no doubt that further changes to the Google algorithm are soon to come. As such, I encourage you to sign up for exclusive updates to take advantage of the free tools, information, and resources as referenced throughout this book via our resources page.

The most important thing to keep in mind as you embark on your journey of optimization is that your success is directly correlated to the understanding and implementation of these SEO techniques. If all you do is read this book, but fail to put into practice the simple techniques you're about to learn, your results won't be any better than they are today. I encourage you to read and do. Keep the long-term goal in mind as you start your journey and you will get there no matter what Google throws your way.

Search Engine Optimization is Still the Holy Grail

The reason search engine optimization continues to be so important is because the data on search marketing and buying behavior has proven time and again that organic search results drive significant amounts of qualified traffic to websites, blogs, and affiliate marketing pages. In fact, studies indicate that 71.3% of searches resulted in a page one Google organic click, not paid. Organic results aren't only clicked on more often, they are also more trusted.

In the last few years, social media, local search, mobile optimization, and personalized browsing experiences that integrate multiple forms of media into a single user session have become commonplace. The culmination of all these factors has resulted in a growing demand for top search engine rankings and a better strategy for achieving number one results or even the coveted 'position zero'.

Many of the individuals and companies I work with through my business, Big Fin SEO, are not only interested in achieving top rankings for their websites, they're also concerned with managing online reputation, gaining a presence through social media, generating multiple listings on page one, and dominating local search. This gives them more real estate on the first page of Google to promote their brands and build brand equity.

This type of need has taken SEO to a completely new level. It used to be that success came from optimizing a single web property but now SEO is really about the optimization of multiple assets (websites, micro-sites, blogs, social media, videos, press releases, review sites, and so on). That's why I felt so compelled to again update this top-selling guide for all those seeking more organic traffic.

Achieving your online goals requires proactive management of online presence in every sense of the word. Knowing the importance of doing so is the first step towards achieving top rankings. With a thorough understanding of search engines, consumer behavior, and the importance of organic search, you're ready to learn SEO techniques that drive results.

I'm often asked whether or not the search engine optimization techniques I first introduced a number of years ago are still valid for optimizing websites and other online assets today. My response to the question is still emphatically "Yes." Not only are the basic techniques effective, they've grown in importance as search engine optimization has evolved over time. And of course, they've been updated to reflect the latest changes in the Google algorithm including all Core updates and even the BERT updated which made a major step towards improving results based on user intent.

In this updated edition, I have refined existing techniques and added new ones that make the most of local search, mobile optimization, social media, content development, achieving position zero, and other recent changes in search. However, the fundamental principals have not changed. Search engines such as Google are still focused on one thing— a positive user experience.

Fast loading websites, valuable content, meaningful interactions, and brand authority, continue to drive search engine results. Sure, the Google algorithm is complicated in some ways, but I'm here to help you with all the particulars. If you start with an understanding that Google values a positive user experience, you're further ahead than most of the so-called SEO experts! Now let's get started...

Special Note: Please share your feedback– good, bad, or indifferent on Amazon.com after reading this book. I'm always looking to improve the quality of information I provide to those interested in SEO (see additional details on page 134) and would love to share some SEO bonuses you won't find anywhere else.

Introduction

If you want to rank on top for Google or other major search engines, you'll need more than just plain luck—you'll need the exact road map used by those who have already achieved top positions for their website(s). That's the purpose of *SEO Made Simple*—to provide you with a simple, easy-to-follow road map for achieving top search engine results for your very own website, blog, or digital assets.

I've personally read dozens of SEO books that left me without any practical advice or the guidance required to improve my website rankings. That was the motivation for this book. You won't find page after page of useless theory here. I wanted to create a helpful guide that would give you enough information to expand your understanding of SEO concepts and ideas, but place more of an emphasis on what to do and how to do it for immediate results that improve your search engine rankings and traffic!

When I started out in Internet marketing no one was able to show me how to achieve the results I was looking for. New to Internet marketing, the prospect of reaching the number one position on Google, or any other website, seemed next to impossible. Of course, there were marketing gurus and tons of Internet marketing products that offered "amazing results" and I tried lots of them. In the end many of these online products didn't live up to expectations. While trying to implement the advice given, I spent thousands of dollars creating and redesigning websites only to find that there was no single solution for getting top rankings on major search engines.

Although discouraged, I never gave up. I knew that in order to be successful online I'd have to increase the natural search engine placements for my website and through a good deal of hard work and persistence, I discovered and refined the search engine optimization secrets I'm going share with you in this book. Now that I've achieved total search engine optimization success through years of trial and error, learning what truly works, I've decided to provide this information to as many individuals as possible seeking online success. Despite popular belief, you won't need an advanced degree in search engine optimization or years of experience in website development to improve your search engine rankings. All you'll need is a desire to have your website ranked number one on Google and a willingness to follow these simple, yet highly effective techniques that have been proven effective again and again.

This is especially important given the continual evolution of Google's algorithm. Today, focusing on things like: content quality, direct and indirect social influence, usage data/traffic and click-through-rate, topical authority, trust and spam metrics, personalization, and user experience (speed and ease) are much more important than ever before SEO is a constantly evolving discipline that is based on a number of core, evergreen principals.

How This Book Is Organized

In thinking about all of this information on SEO and how to present it, I decided to organize this book into two main sections: *On-Page Optimization* and *Off-Page Optimization*. Each section is designed to help you understand and implement the same techniques I've used to achieve top search engine placements for my own sites and the websites of hundreds of clients.

Section 1: On-Page Optimization

The first section is an introduction to search engines and fundamental search engine optimization (SEO) techniques. On-page optimization covers everything you should do when developing your website and web pages. Don't worry if you've already spent money on designing your website or have limited knowledge of HTML or even website development itself. Once you learn these effective techniques and understand how to use them, they can be applied in just a matter of minutes to any new or existing website.

Surprisingly, many of these techniques are overlooked by 95 percent of all Internet marketers and those who are attempting to improve their search engine result placements (SERPs). How do I know? Because when my company reviews websites for clients, many of them aren't applying these powerful SEO techniques.

At the end of this section, I'll provide a summary of the most important points covered concerning on-page optimization. You can use the summary page for quick review or as an ongoing reference to simplify your optimization efforts.

Section 2: Off-Page Optimization

The second section focuses on external factors that affect your Google ranking. With recent changes to the Google algorithm the focus has evolved to balance the importance of both on-page and off-page factors. You still need to start with and rely on onsite optimization but also need to focus on applying off-page optimization techniques. These are largely focused on attracting quality inbound links to your website. Off page techniques are among the most powerful and effective for improving your search engine results. In this section, I'll discuss off-page optimization and reveal the same strategies I use on a daily basis to increase website rankings. After applying these techniques in combination with on-page optimization, your website ranking will literally begin to skyrocket toward the top of Google and other major search engines.

It's important to note that off-page optimization is covered in the second section of this book because without on-page optimization factors being implemented correctly, your website can never achieve top placement (OK, *never* is an exaggeration but it would take much longer and require greater effort).

Again, at the end of this section I'll provide a summary of its most important points for quick reference.

Section 3: Research to Practice

In this section I'm going to show you how to manage your website optimization efforts on a daily and weekly basis. This simple process keeps your website moving higher in search results and ensures that it stays there! Applying these techniques is the key to achieving results and protecting your top search positions.

Section 4: SEO Glossary

The final section of this book contains an updated SEO glossary that can serve as a helpful reference along your search engine optimization journey. By understanding key phrases and SEO language, you're sure to reach your final destination.

SEO Made Simple provides exactly what you need to begin your climb to the number one search position on Google, just as I have for many of my websites and blogs, and the websites I've developed and optimized for a long list of high-profile customers. As each page unfolds, and you learn the most powerful techniques for search engine optimization, you will achieve search engine success!

The Beginning

When I started learning about SEO, I really didn't know where to begin. And like most stories of challenge, I was at my wit's end—I had tried everything. After many sleepless nights, nearly $20,000 wasted on website development with nothing to show for it, I was tired, frustrated, and broke. But I had to keep going.

I'd already made a considerable effort to improve website rankings and knew there were others getting success in this area. Quitting was not an option for me. I began studying what other successful SEO's were doing and began applying what I learned to my own website. Before long, I was seeing significant improvements in my organic search results – driving tons of qualified visitors to my websites and blogs. **These findings resulted in what I am now calling the *SEO Made Simple* method.** My focus was and still is Google because it garners more search traffic than all other search engines combined. I've also learned that the optimization techniques used to reach number one on the world's largest search engine are unique and continue to evolve. Now in its 7th edition, *SEO Made Simple* reflects all of the changes and updates to my most effective optimization techniques.

Did you know?

According to recent studies, the top three natural search results on Google receive more than 70 percent of all search engine clicks!

After spending many late nights applying the SEO techniques I learned, it wasn't long before I developed faster, more efficient ways of getting results. These optimization techniques saved me valuable time and money, making the process much easier and faster to implement. I'll be sharing all of these techniques with you in the pages that follow so you can avoid wasting endless hours on manual processes that can easily be automated.

As a quick aside, let me show you the power of applying *SEO Made Simple* techniques from some of today's leading content providers. Search engine optimization is all about optimizing your site for a given keyword or phrase. We'll be talking about keywords later in this book, but for now, all you need to know is that when you visit Google and search for something, the words you enter are comprised of either a single word or phrase. These words are called a *search term* or *keyword*.

Let's take the following example. Go to Google and type, *"marketing articles"*. Somewhere near the top you'll find a listing from Hubspot titled, "The 9 Best Marketing Articles of All Time, According to HubSpot". At the time of this writing, how has Hubspot outranked 'Entrepreneur' and 'The New York Times' for this highly competitive keyword? Why do they appear in the first position when it comes to this somewhat obscure search term? The answer is rather simple. They've become the authority on all-things marketing related. As a result, Google favors them in search results.

There are tons of other, more technical factors that explain why Hubspot ranks first for this particular search phrase. And we'll explore them all as I break down the individual optimization criteria that determine ranking. For now, the key takeaway is that Google sees Hubspot as an authority on this topic. They've made the determination based on more than 200 documented factors in their algorithm which has been reinforced by user behavior. They know, based on the number of unique people searching for the keyword phrase, "marketing articles" and clicking on the Hubspot result that people are finding what they're looking for. It's basically the best answer to the user's search query.

When I say best, that's a loaded phrase. The machine called Google has made this distinction based on specific inputs in relation to all of the other potential search results. In SEO, sometimes it's about being slightly better than your competition – not always being perfect.

The good news is that as you begin apply some basic SEO techniques, you'll start to see improvements in your organic traffic. This may be due to weak competition or simply paying attention to details that others have missed. I've been able to achieve top placements using the techniques I'll be revealing throughout the first few sections of this book. I've also successfully ranked hundreds of client sites for competitive terms by applying SEO best practices better than their nearest competition.

The best part of SEO is that I don't spend a single penny on Google Adwords or any other type of online advertising. Why would I? I'm getting all the traffic I can handle from the number one placement on the largest search engine in the world for keywords I can monetize. The same is true for other sites I optimize. Said plainly, nothing beats top rankings for targeted search terms.

One of the most important aspects of organic traffic is the "trust factor". After years of using Google Search, consumers can clearly distinguish between paid advertising and organic results. Within a split second, they decide if it's worth clicking on an ad or choosing a more objective result. Focusing your effort on organic results, the more trusted listing, is always the best way to go.

Research has shown that users generally prefer organic rankings, about 7 out of 10. As buyer intent changes, the goal of the purchaser, they become more comfortable with clicking on ads but will certainly have their guard up. As a result, once you master organic search, you may want to supplement your efforts with paid advertising. One of the techniques I share in this book is combining organic and paid opportunities on Google to ensure the majority of traffic comes your way.

Based on a recent study of nearly 5 million users, Backlinko discovered the number one result in Google's organic search results gets clicked 31.7% of the time. Additionally, organic click-through-rate (CTR) for positions 7-10 is virtually the same. What does it all mean? It means that getting your website listed in the top 3 search results can literally transform your business and should be your primary goal. The more relevant your website, blog post, or content, the more clicks and website visitor you'll receive.

The next time you go to Google and do a search, realize what the engine is trying to accomplish for the user - answering their question quickly, confidently, and with utmost clarity. They don't want users conducting multiple searches or reading through hundreds of results to find answers. Sometimes this means users will find answers without having to click through on a search result. In other situations it means providing a variety of result formats to choose from such as blog articles, reference sites, or videos. Regardless, we know that users want answers, and they want them quickly. Having your website listed at the top of a search results page makes it much more likely to be the resource they choose.

I've reached top placements on Google with a basic understanding of SEO, developing insights into Google intent, and discovering powerful SEO tools that give me an unbelievable edge over the competition. Now it's your turn. Let's begin with a basic understanding of Google so you can discover how to play the game of top rankings and win.

What You Need to Know about Google

Google's the biggest—make no mistake about it. According to the most recent data, Google has 90.46% of the search engine market share worldwide. That's basically all of it! And new search queries are being created all the time. In fact, more than 15% of all searches have never been searched before on Google. Google receives over 63,000 searches per second on any given day. You could call them the nine-hundred pound gorilla.

Here are some general Google data points you should know as reported by Wordstream:

- 3.5 billion Google searches are made every day. (Internet Live Stats)

- The volume of Google searches grows by roughly 10% every year. (Internet Live Stats)

- Every year, somewhere between 16% and 20% of Google searches are new—they've never been searched before. (Internet Live Stats)

- 90% of searches made on desktops are done via Google. (Statista)

- 35% of product searches start on Google. (eMarketer)

Google Ranking

What makes Google unique compared to other search engines, in addition to its size, is their proprietary website-ranking algorithm. Previously, this ranking algorithm could be summed up with a single metric called Google PageRank or Google PR. Named after one of Google's founders, Larry Page, Google PR was symbolic of the SEO industry. Google Page Rank is no longer valid due to the growing complexity of the algorithm and advancements in artificial intelligence but the premise of being able to evaluate your website objectively is still very appealing for those trying to improve rankings. At the end of the day, we want to know how our website compares to those we're competing against. We also want to make sure that we are doing everything we can to beat Google at its own rankings game. Fortunately for us, there are a number of ways to do so.

In order to improve rankings, you need to see how your website measures up. There are a variety of SEO tools and resources that can help you do this. One powerful resource is Moz which uses measures like MozRank and MozTrust to assess the overall health and relevance of your website. Other popular tools such as SEMrush and ahrefs have similar measures and offer very sophisticated platforms for SEOs working to optimize client websites.

Measures like mozRank and mozTrust have such an appeal because they were designed to help answer the question, "What can I do to make my website better in the eyes of Google?" Regardless of which metric you choose to believe in, the concept of SEO metrics are important to understand. They give you a sense of how Google views a website from a technical and non-technical perspective, which helps explain why we rank the way we do.

Why does Google return one result over another? It begins by assigning a weight or level of importance to a given web page. This weight is determined by a variety of factors which we cover throughout this guide. Personally, I like to think of it as a voting system.

Imagine that Google search results are based on a huge election where users and machines cast votes for one another. Those votes are based on how well you conform to on-site factors like page titles, page descriptions, etc., off-site factors like who links to your website, and other factors dealing with how well your site performs for people using it.

One of the more talked about criterion affecting rankings is the coveted in-bound link. For example, every time a website links to another website, they cast a "vote." The more votes an individual site receives, the more important they must be and the higher the site appears in search results! Seems pretty simple, right? Well…sort of, but not exactly.

In addition to weighing website factors (a.k.a. on page optimization) Google doesn't treat all inbound links the same. You see, in this special election, not all votes are created equal—some votes hold more weight than others. For example, if an authoritative website places a vote for a new website, that vote theoretically counts more than a vote from a website with less authority. The harsh reality is that votes from different voters are weighted differently.

Said another way, it's not just the vote you're looking for—you also want a vote from the "right" person. In this instance, the "right" person is a website with lots of influence. In my opinion, you're better off generating fewer links from sites that are more authoritative than many sites that have low relevance or authority.

Whether you're looking at inbound links, on page optimization, or other factors – which we cover throughout this guide, it all comes down to how your site is viewed by Google which is a complex algorithm that measures your site based on SEO best practices.

Google Evolves

It's important to understand how Google search results have evolved so you can understand where things are headed. Sometimes effective SEO is simply about staying ahead of the curve and being prepared for what's next. Back in the day when this all began, search was relatively simple. Buy a URL with your keyword in it and top rankings were virtually guaranteed. Over the past number of years however, Google has been focused on improving the search experience and has added a layer of complexity to search engine rankings like never before. In addition to penalizing sites for using inappropriate optimization techniques, they've simultaneously enhanced the search experience for those browsing the web. This has created a significant difference in how people use search engines and the results they see in their custom feed.

User intent. Thanks to artificial intelligence and machine learning, Google has cracked the code on user intent. Without getting too technical, Google has enough data to figure out what you're looking for, even before you do. Some may call it mind reading, but I call it a seamless user experience. Looking for, "restaurants near me"? Well, if you favor Italian, you'll probably have more of them listed in search results thanks to the reviews you left on various apps and Google maps tracking the restaurants you've already visited. Want to figure out how to screw in a light bulb? Well, if you usually watch videos on how to do fixer-upper projects, you'll probably see Youtube videos in your search results too. Google knows what content you consume and how often. Looking to get from point A to point B? You might find Google maps popping up on your phone if it's your preferred navigator with time to destination prominently displayed.

How is this all possible? Data and machines. Google knows what you're looking for and gets better every second of every day. They're not just looking at you, but billions and billions of search behaviors all over the world. With each keystroke or tap, they collect more information, making your search experience more intuitive. They are getting a clearer understanding between what an individual does – the keywords they use, the websites they visit, the apps they prefer, etc. and what results matter to them as measured with clicks, time on screen, and engagement. Today, people don't just get their content from a webpage, it's much more complex. Given so many devices and different types of media, access to data has never been so important and meaningful.

Universal search. With the advent of video, blogs, podcasts, real-time social media, and countless apps, Google has enhanced the search experience for all of us. A typical page of search results may include a popular video from YouTube, a news feed from a leading news site, and relevant reviews or product images. Even local businesses have received a boost thanks to the Google My Business directory.

All of this may feel a bit frenetic, but it does create a more robust experience for those using Google. However, it also requires proactive management for anyone interested in SEO to promote their website, business, or online reputation. Search engine optimization has become less about getting a single site ranked in the number one position and more about acquiring multiple listings on a search results page for relevant searches. Do a Google search on "bmw auto" to see universal search results in action.

If you're searching on your phone, you'll probably see location specific results including dealers near you, ads, and much more. If you're using a desktop, you'll probably see bmw's for sale, images, ads, resource sites, and even a Google Answer Box. What is a Google Answer box? Google's answer box is a unique search engine result, powered by the knowledge graph or scraped from a site that provides an adequate answer. It's typically displayed at the top of the results page, but below ads. SEO's call this position zero. Many of our clients want this position only to learn that it doesn't have much of a positive impact on website traffic. None-the-less, it does add a few clicks to the mix and can help a brand building campaign.

Due to the advent of universal search, and focus on local, search engine optimization has changed dramatically. Instead of just optimizing for a single website, I recommend applying all the techniques you'll learn in this book to any digital asset including things like press releases, social media profiles, videos, images, etc.

The more assets you optimize, the greater your presence on search result pages for a given keyword phrase. This takes additional effort but not much additional knowledge. When you understand the basics of search engine optimization you can use slight modifications to optimize virtually anything online.

Mobile First. Mobile-first indexing is exactly what it sounds like. It just means the mobile version of your website becomes the starting point for what Google includes in their index, and the baseline for how they determine rankings. It's called "mobile-first" because it's not a mobile-only index. For example, if a site doesn't have a mobile-friendly version, the desktop site can still be included in the index. But the lack of a mobile-friendly experience negatively impacts your rankings and a site with a better mobile experience would potentially receive a rankings boost even for searchers on a desktop.

Lucky for us, most website platforms from Wix to WordPress are developed in a mobile responsive way. Regardless of the device being used to browse the web, your site content is configured properly. I mention mobile first to give you a sense of what matters most when considering search engine results.

Google updates. Upgrades to the Google algorithm have enhanced the user experience from start to finish. Google suggest which recommends search terms as you type your query in both search and Gmail, updates to Google My Business, mobile first indexing, and a significant leap forward in user intent thanks to the BERT update, means that users can access information more quickly and more precisely than previously thought possible.

Understanding how Google has evolved is essential to getting and keeping your website ranked in the top positions for chosen keywords. It might feel overwhelming at the moment, but as we dissect the different ways to drive qualified traffic to your business, the easier it becomes. In addition, Google offers many tools to help you along the way.

Google Search Console

Google is one of the most innovative companies on the planet. They actually want you to succeed. Why? It's because Google exists to improve search. To support this mission Google has developed a number of tools you can use to "improve" your online search experience and website.

Visit https://search.google.com/search-console to view these helpful web tools.

If your website is new, register with Google Search Console. I strongly recommend checking out the education Google offers. It's very helpful information for using Google Console and optimizing your website. Once you've accessed the platform, you'll be able to:

- **Get Google's view of your website and diagnose potential problems.** See how Google crawls and indexes your site and learn about specific problems Google has accessing it.

- **Discover your link and query traffic.** View, classify, and download comprehensive data about internal and external links to your site with new link reporting tools. Find out which Google search queries drive traffic to your site, and see exactly how users arrive there.

- **Share information about your site.** Tell Google about your pages with Sitemaps: which ones are the most important to you and how often they change. You can also let us know how you would like the URLs we index to appear.

It always amazes me how few people actually use Google Search Console despite its importance. Sometimes people are so fixated on Google Analytics, they lose sight of this Google Tool which is designed specifically for SEO. If you do nothing else while reading this guide, sign up for Google Search Console and verify your site. Once you've reviewed all of the issues that Google suggests you remedy, I strongly suggest you upload an XML sitemap to your account. This is essential for Google to easily and fully crawl your website. Once your site is properly indexed it can be appropriately ranked for suggested keywords. If you need help with any of these features, visit the Big Fin SEO resources page or search do-it-yourself Google videos on YouTube.

I'll go into more details later about sitemaps, but "yes", they are still used today and important to create for both your site and Google Search Console. At the time of this writing there's a great free tool you can use to generate an html sitemap and xml sitemap with the click of a button. Visit https://www.xml-sitemaps.com/ to learn more.

If you are more advanced and would like to look at additional data associated with your site, I encourage you to tag the site with Google Analytics code. There are complete books on Google analytics (GA) so I won't go into here, but adding tracking code may also provide additional insights for your SEO and site performance. It's extremely easy to use and has become the standard for website analytics. Best of all, it's completely free!

Personally, I use Google Analytics and Google Search Console on a regular basis. The data and insights provided are extremely helpful in understanding why your site ranks well or why it doesn't. The data also gives insight into who is coming to your site, where they go, and how they leave. It's like having x-ray vision, seeing exactly what's good and bad about your website. If you don't know how to implement either of these, reach out to the online community or hire a freelancer online to install the code for you and get your site verified. Sites like Upwork.com provide skilled programmers for as little as $10/hr.

Now that you know about the world's largest search engine and some tools they offer, it's time to begin improving your website's Google ranking. Let's get started!

Section 1

On-Page Optimization

On-Page Optimization

As I mentioned in the introduction, there are essentially two parts to any SEO effort: on-page optimization and off-page optimization. We begin with an overview and deep dive covering on-page optimization because it creates the foundation for your SEO and is pretty easy to understand. Basically, on-page optimization is what you do on your web pages that can have a positive or negative impact on search engine results — where your site is ranked on Google for a particular search term or phrase.

What Is On-Page Optimization?

Defined in its most simple form, on-page optimization is what you do on your website to help or hurt your search engine result page (SERPs). From my perspective, on-page optimization also refers to critical planning steps like understanding your niche, keyword research, and website strategy.

The best part of on-page optimization is that it's fully in your control. If done correctly it can improve how search engines see your website, weigh your relevant content (keywords), and place your website within search results for a given term. This is especially true for local and mobile search results.

Many Internet marketers debate the importance of on-page optimization when it comes to Google. I believe the effects of on-page optimization are paramount given the latest changes to the Google algorithm which are looking for natural language and targeted content. Any serious Google optimization effort cannot be effective unless on-page optimization is thoroughly addressed at the start of any search engine optimization campaign.

What I'm referring to when I speak about specific on-page optimization factors is the proper use of *meta tags*, *website URLs*, *formatting, internal linking and friendly URLs*, *keyword development*, and *on-page placement.* Let's review each item in detail after you learn about the importance of keyword research. I'll show you step-by-step what you need to know to ensure that your web pages are 100 percent optimized for Google.

Warning: Once you update your site with the proper on-page optimization tactics, you might very quickly find yourself starting to improve ranking for a variety of keywords.

Keyword Research

The more I learn about search engine optimization, the more I've come to rely on effective keyword research. Finding the search phrases that your website or blog should be optimized for is essential to any search engine optimization campaign. The goal is to find relevant, high traffic keywords that will be less competitive from an optimization perspective. Less competition means that you'll have a much better chance of achieving number one rankings for your chosen keyword phrase. Doing this takes a little work but is well worth it.

The value of selecting keywords strategically is very high. The "right" keywords allow your optimization efforts to happen quicker and produce the best organic result. Many of the companies I've consulted for over the past few years didn't pay much attention to keyword research. As a result, they were either trying to optimize websites for keywords they could never achieve number one rankings for, because an authority site like Amazon held the top position, or for keywords that had next to no search volume.

Not too long ago I had a conversation with a potential client. We were introduced through a mutual friend and sat down to dinner to discuss his online marketing needs. I started to ask him questions about his online marketing strategy, website, and so on. About thirty minutes into the conversation, he said, "I don't need SEO. I'm already ranked number one." When I asked him what keyword he was ranking for, I looked it up on my mobile web browser. I wanted to see how much search volume this particular keyword phrase had on a monthly basis.

Not surprisingly, the keyword that he was so enthusiastic about was getting less than thirty searches per month. That's it! It's pretty difficult to build a multi-million dollar business on only thirty searches a month, especially considering that not all the clicks go to the top ranked result, only about 30%. He was surprised and said, "But in my industry that's how everyone refers to our service." I responded with, "That's clearly not the case given the low search volume."

After we started working together, I showed him the proper way to do keyword research and find the actual keyword phrases that people in his industry were typing into Google to find services like the ones he was offering. With thorough research we found keywords his website could realistically rank well for in a short amount of time and also had enough traffic to sustain and grow his business.

Keyword Development and Placement

Keyword development is one of the most important optimization factors you'll learn about and can make or break your website's ranking. But don't let that scare you. I'll be showing you the best way to find the right keywords and determine whether or not you can rank well for them.

Why are keywords so important? Because search engine algorithms are largely based on keywords and keyword phrases—keywords on your web page, keywords in your code, keywords in the links within and pointing to your website or blog. I guess you could say that Google has keywords on the brain. Their goal is to return websites and other digital assets that most closely align with a user's search query. This is why keywords are so important to get right.

A keyword is any word or phrase that describes your website and/or web page content. Another way to think about it is in the form of a search term. What a user enters into the Google search box is considered a *keyword* or *keyword phrase*.

A number of years ago, Google started helping searchers by implementing Google Suggest – still in effect today. Google Suggest is the feature producing suggested search terms as you begin typing into the search engine's search bar. Enter a query like, "kitten" and you're likely to see suggested terms including, "kitten for sale", "kitten near me", and "kitten adoption". Additionally, Google Suggest will offer up some local terms you may want to consider as well. Google Suggest is both a blessing and a curse when it comes to SEO. Using Google Suggest to help find frequently searched keywords can be a valuable part of your optimization strategy.

Before get too deep into keyword research, let me begin by saying that choosing a keyword phrase is more art than science. However, your selection of a keyword can be greatly simplified if you follow these steps:

1. **Define the content of your site in general terms.** What is my site about? Tennis shoes? Photography? Business services? Desserts? Once you've identified a general topic, it's time to start your keyword research.

2. **Identify keywords/keyword phrases related to your topic.** To do so, visit Google Adwords. If you don't have an Adwords account, you will need to sign up for one at:

https://ads.google.com/home. It's free and will begin to get you familiar with a variety of Google ad tools. In the Tools & Settings area, located on the top navigation, you'll find the *Keyword Planner* tool.

You may be asking why we would use an Adwords tool for SEO, but you'll quickly discover the power of this free resource that provides search volumes and suggested keyword phrases.

3. **Select Discover New Keywords.** Enter your product or service, the website URL, or a product category and press *Get Results*. The list of ad groups and keywords shown contain all of the search terms and search counts—the number of searches using that keyword or keyword phrase performed during a given month on Google. Results are sorted by relevance but can also be sorted by search volume or competition.

   Personally I like to start with the URL search under the "Start with a website" tab. I enter the website of the three biggest competitors in my space and download all of Google's suggested keywords.

4. **Select anywhere from ten to thirty keyword phrases to research further.** OK, here is where the rubber meets the road. Look at your list and choose a few *keyword phrases* (not an individual word because, in most instances, it will be way too competitive with many sites trying to rank high for that particular keyword) that accurately represent your website. Make sure your phrases have a search volume of at least seven hundred monthly searches unless you are in a very small niche. Keep in mind that the more searches on a given keyword, the more competitive it may be. Eliminate keywords with 10,000 or more searches per month.

   Now you might be asking, "Why NOT pick the phrase with the greatest number of searches?" It stands to reason that the greater the number of searches, the greater number of visitors to your website. However, there are other factors to consider such as how competitive it will be to rank well for the given search term.

   When I conduct keyword research I usually generate a short list by eliminating anything over ten thousand searches per month unless supporting a recognized brand and anything less than seven or eight hundred searches per month. I also eliminate phrases that appear unnatural or may be difficult to use in a sentence. This simple method usually gets my list down to about thirty keywords or so. Then I go to the next step to refine my search further.

5. **SEO Competitiveness.** Your ability to rank well is not just dependent on search volume for specific keywords. In fact, it's even more important to find keywords that drive qualified traffic to your website or blog and are not extremely competitive. I've had a number of clients over the years who did their own keyword research only to struggle for page one rankings. Where they went wrong was choosing keywords based on search volume alone.

   When using the Google Adwords Keyword Planner tool you'll see a "Competition" column. What this refers to is the advertising competition for a keyword. Over the years, I have found that low competition on Adwords generally reflects less competition in organic search but not always. Remember, you're looking for well trafficked keywords that are easy to rank for – at least easier than some of the more competitive search phrases others are trying to rank for.

   Take your list of thirty or so keyword phrases and evaluate their SEO competitiveness either by looking at the Adwords competition or, more effectively, by using the Moz SEO keyword research tool or plugin. There are other resources available such as SEMrush that can help you in this regard. If you do not have access to these tools, start with a free trial or search for an online coupon. Don't be afraid to try them. Mastering these tools gets easier by the day as they continue to develop new features. There are always new tools coming on the market to give you this type of information at a lower cost, so don't hesitate to experiment with free tools that offer SEO competition information as well as on page insights.

   Keywords that have high SEO competition aren't there by happenstance. As more websites build content around certain terms, they become more competitive. This means ranking well for a particular keyword may take time, website authority, and lots of optimization to achieve. Your best bet is to choose keywords most closely aligned to your website with the least amount of SEO competition.

I also like to look at the number of competing sites/pages simply by searching for your keyword phrase in Google and looking at the total number of results noted in the upper left-hand corner of the search results page under the search box.

For example, if we were to choose the keyword phrase *womens tennis shoes* and do a search in Google, we would see that 917,410,000 web pages (at time of publication) contain the phrase *womens tennis shoes*. Not only that, but looking at the results, I see all of the major shoe brands from NIKE to Zappos. Looks like I'd need to expand my keyword search to find something less competitive.

Depending on my initial research, I may choose to look at expanded phrases or phrases related more specifically to what I'm selling. "Popular tennis shoes for women", "Green tennis shoes for women", etc. By having more specific phrases that are less competitive, I stand a much better chance of top rankings. Add in local search intent and your chances of generating organic traffic go up exponentially.

One great way to do this is with the "People also ask" feature that appears for a number of Google Searches. It's always a good idea to type your target keywords into an actual Google Search to see what else is popular via the Google Suggest tool and the "People also ask" accordion if one is available in search results.

6. **Research the competition.** Regardless of which tool you use to generate or research keyword phrases, you'll need to size up your competition. This is the final step in keyword research and definitely one of the most important when it comes to developing a strong list of potential keywords to optimize for. Remember that Google is a voting machine. The question you need to ask yourself is whether or not you can optimize your website (both on-page and off) better than your competition and attract more votes! If you can, you'll quickly find yourself at the top of search engine results. This step is extremely important so we'll take a deeper dive on the most effective way to research your competition. Again, I like to use SEMrush or the Moz plugin to automate a lot of this work and confirm my research with actual data.

Don't skip this step. As I mentioned previously, achieving your SEO goals is more about beating out the competition than being perfect when it comes to implementing SEO techniques. The more you know about your competitors, the more you learn about your own business and how you should be attacking your SEO.

Researching the Competition

Researching the top-performing websites for final selection of your keyword phrase is the most important step in keyword selection and it takes a little work. The good news is that Firefox and Google Chrome have a variety of plugins or add-ons you can use to make your final analysis a lot easier. Plugins like Moz and SEOquake provide much of the on-page analysis quickly, as opposed to doing all of your research manually—thank goodness!

After you've narrowed down your keyword list to just a handful of terms, the next step is researching the competition. I will now show you how to research the competition using a real-world example so you can do it for your own website. You should learn how to research your competition on your own to better understand this process of choosing keywords before using some of the automated tools previously mentioned. Doing so is analogous to learning division longhand before you start using a calculator!

Picking up on our earlier example, assume you've selected a primary keyword phrase and have decided to begin researching the competitors (ex: *womens tennis shoes*).

1. **Visit Google and enter the first keyword phrase you are researching.** Search the keyword phrase "womens tennis shoes".

2. **Identify the natural search results versus the paid search results**. The natural results will appear below any paid results.

Write down the URLs of the first set of organic search results. The URLs will appear in green beneath each description. In this example, let's imagine the first few natural results are:

- https://www.tennis-warehouse.com/Tennis_Shoes_Women.html

- https://www.dickssportinggoods.com/products/tennis-shoes-for-women.jsp

- https://www.nike.com/w/womens-tennis-shoes-5e1x6zed1qzy7ok

Before going any further, I like to do a quick look-see to determine the overall competitiveness in search results of the keyword I'm researching. If you're using one of the plugins noted above, all you have to do is look at the domain strength, page authority, or other stat relating to the overall site ranking to determine how your site compares – each tool provides a slightly different authority metric. If sites listed in the top few positions are highly authoritative, then your chances of top rankings for your particular keyword are slim. You'll learn more about these metrics throughout this guide.

Here are a few things to look for as your review the top listings with or without a competitive plugin: Are the search result listings from competitive sites like "Amazon", "Facebook", "Sneaker.com", etc.? Are the sites appearing in the top positions strong brand names? Are the results to root domains (ex: www.womanstennisshoes.com) or are they from pages that reside lower on a domain? What I'm looking for is what I call "authority factors". If sites ranking for the keywords are large, authoritative, well promoted websites, your chances of ranking for that particular keyword are less than ideal.

3. **Now you're ready to begin your site-by-site analysis.**

    Begin by installing an SEO browser add-on. As mentioned previously, this could be the Moz plugin on Chrome, the SEOquake plugin on Firefox or a free resource like https://www.seoptimer.com. If none of these options work for you, search for an SEO tool using Google and simply choose one. The goal is to use a free tool to evaluate not only your website (which we'll do later), but your primary competitors. Without a goal, it's hard to know what you should be focusing your SEO effort on when it comes time for optimizing your own website.

    For this example, I'm going to use the SEOquake plugin. What we need to do is analyze the following for each site to determine if you can outrank them. I can show you how to do the first one— then simply repeat the same steps for sites two, three, four, and five. For each site, begin by recording the following:

    - Website URL

    - Website authority (Domain authority)

- Number of sites linking in

- Website age

- On page factors

These are just a few of the items to consider but let's do this for first result, tennis warehouse. Keep in mind that your browsing results may differ slightly.

Begin by recording the URL of this site. I like to use an excel spreadsheet. Remember, I'm showing you how to do this manually so you fully understand the process. But you only have to do this once. Moving forward, we'll let our automated tools do the work for us. The next step is to identify the authority of the website or webpage being listed in search results (using Moz, or SEOquake, or free SEO crawler, etc.). According to my tool, looks like Tennis Warehouse has a Domain Score of 34 and a Trust Score of 40. Not bad! Even though the metrics are slightly lower than the number 2 and number 3 results, they're strong enough to justify a top ranking.

The second thing we need to do is evaluate other factors such as age and size of site (pages indexed). This particular listing has been around since 1998. It partly explains why they maintain the top spot. The older and larger the website, the more authority it commands. As sites become authoritative, they have more meaning to Google and will rank for a broader set of keywords. For example, if you are trying to rank your new blog for "women's tennis shoes" and the number one ranking is Amazon, don't bother. You could never build enough site authority to outrank Amazon.com. Rather, focus on other keywords that Amazon is not competing for. Perhaps something like "classic Nike tennis shoes size 8". Not only will you do better organically, but you will receive more targeted traffic with purchase intent.

I also see 3.9k inbound links to this particular webpage. Wow, talk about a vote of confidence. Google doesn't have to look far to determine just how the voting audience of the world wide web feels about Tennis Warehouse. Maybe I need to stop buying my shoes off of Amazon.

Other on-page optimization factors, like the ones we discuss in the on-page optimization section such as meta tags, use of <h1> tags, keyword use, and so on, influence organic rankings. If your site is on par with others in search results from an age, authority, inbound link perspective, and overall website size, consider additional on page factors that can help to differentiate your site and help you rank better in Google.

For example, I recommend looking at on-page factors like keyword usage – is the keyword found in the meta data (meta title, description, and keywords), on the page in a header such as an <h1>, <h2>, and <h3> tag, does it appear in content, does the keyword phrase appear in towards the beginning, do alt image tags include your keyword? By thoroughly evaluating all of these factors, and more we'll cover, you can determine just how well optimized a particular competitor may be. If sites are not well optimized, it may be an opportunity for you to compete effectively on the chose keyword.

So what have we learned about this site? Based on my analysis, it appears as though Tennis Warehouse is extremely authoritative but not the most authoritative site on the topic of women's tennis shoes. Yet they command the top spot for this keyword search. How can that be? I use this particular website as an early example to illustrate that SEO is based on a variety of factors, but top rankings may come down to just a few. I know from deep research on this particular site that due to the site's age, click-through rates (from search results to website), and referring websites, they have a distinct advantage over the big boys like Nike and Dick's Sporting Goods. Said another way, you don't have to be a brand name to score big with SEO. Tennis Warehouse was one of the first sites to sell women's tennis shoes online and has been benefiting from their early entry for the last couple of decades. In addition, their site is highly responsive and passes many of the technical SEO checks that others do not.

Now you might be thinking, "I've got a new website how can I compete?" Well, that's the benefit of keyword and competitor research. The more you investigate those in the top positions, the more you learn about developing an effective SEO strategy. Choosing the right keywords can mean the difference between success and failure. Add the proper application of optimization techniques and you could very quickly find yourself showing up for a variety of competitive keyword phrases.

Keyword Research Shortcut

Now that you've seen the step-by-step process for keyword research, I'd like to share with you another example for determining keyword competitiveness that's easy to do. Just like any good search engine optimization expert, my methods for reviewing and optimizing websites is constantly changing and improving. However, the same basic fundamentals still apply. Here is another method to quickly determine the competitiveness of a particular keyword. I like to call it a 'snap shot' view of your competition.

This method simply asks you to do a Google Search for your keyword phrase and view the search result listings from the perspective of *Universal Search* and *Authority*. In the following example the keyword phrase being analyzed is "things to do in lima peru". Our goal is to look at the results to determine the type of listings, such as websites, answer box, videos, images, press releases, etc., and the authority of each site. This gives us a much better understanding of all the ways we could show up in search results. So often we think in basic ways that we limit ourselves.

In this example, these listings look pretty solid – Google answer boxes, ads, and top websites like Tripadvisor.com, TripSavvy, etc. Now, let's compare this to a popular destination in Peru like the "Pisac Market".

In this example, we see a dynamic set of results for our target keyword. This list, which is a combination of websites, blogs, videos, rating sites, answer boxes, etc., would be slightly easier to rank for as it's a true combination of different types of websites and digital assets which are less authoritative. The dynamic nature, and lack of as many authority sites in our example, means that you'll have an easier time ranking for the second keyword phrase "Pisa market" than you would the first.

Once you've narrowed down your list based on your understanding of the market, search volumes, intent, and competitiveness, do the final and easiest step, taking a snap-shot view of your competitors via the search result listings (SERPs) using SEOquake or the Moz plugin. If results are dynamic in nature and you see few authoritative sites, then you've found the perfect keyword to optimize for.

One of the questions I frequently get is, "What if all of the results are authoritative? What should I do then?" The answer is to keep looking. You can obviously try to optimize for a competitive keyword phrase that has strong competition but why? There are billions of keyword phrases, maybe even trillions available. And you won't know unless you do the research. If you've hit a roadblock, go back to Google Adwords to find additional phrases or a combination of a branded term (including the name of your company or website) and non-branded terms. Doing the proper research up front, finding and optimizing for a phrase that is less competitive, will put you ahead of 99.9% of other websites and improve your organic results.

Now that you understand the fundamentals of keyword research, let's focus on creating a well optimized site from an on-page optimization perspective using your target keywords. That's why we start with keyword research and then on-page optimization. Optimizing your "on page" factors without knowing what keywords you're targeting is never productive.

Bonus: After searching for your keyword phrase, scroll all the way to the bottom of search results and consider related search terms lists.

On Page Factors

Now that you've learned the process of keyword research, the next step is to understand the factors that are involved in proper on-page optimization and some off-page. Armed with this knowledge, you can apply the right keywords needed for optimizing your website, blogs, affiliate landing pages and other online assets, resulting in a quick rise to the top.

Let's start with important on-page optimization strategies essential for any well positioned website. You can manage many of these on-page factors using your website editor, plugin, or html editor. If you don't have access to your site's web pages or lack HTML experience, you can outsource this work but still need a basic understanding of what to do and how to do it. I cover everything you need to know about outsourcing later in this book so take a deep breath and relax. Effective search engine optimization is actually easier than you think.

As a quick side note, let me emphasize the importance of having direct access to your website. Many of the clients I've worked with over the past decade have to contact someone, usually with whom they haven't spoken with in a year or more to get access to their own website. The days of abdicating responsibility for your website are long gone. Remember, it's your responsibility to have ownership over your own website – it's the lifeblood of your business. I'm not saying you have to do all the work yourself, or any of it for that matter, but you should always be able to log into the back end of your website and access your hosting account at a minimum.

You can easily gain control of your site by visiting your webhost (ex: Godaddy) and getting all of your login credentials. All of these sites have very helpful customer support if you don't know how to find the information you need.

Meta Tags

A meta tag is any one of a variety of labels you give your web page. There are quite a number of different meta tags but we'll only be discussing the most common ones here. These "tags" or labels are essential for helping search engines understand the name of your website's pages, what information the pages contain, are used to display a small description for search engine result listings, and determine how best to treat each page when indexed.

Meta tags are important because different search engines weigh the information in these tags differently. It is believed that Google uses meta tags in relation to other factors, ensuring consistency and validating key metrics about page content. It's good practice to make sure that your meta tags are complete, accurate, and up-to-date.

Note: **Each page found on your website must have its own unique set of meta tags. Duplicate tags will harm your rankings.**

Here's an example of the home page meta tags I use to describe just one of my websites, BigFinSEO.com:

> \<**title**\>Big Fin SEO | Affordable Search Engine Optimization\</**title**\>
> \<meta name="**Description**" content="Big Fin SEO is a search engine optimization service that helps companies improve website visibility and ranking by using only the latest SEO strategies."\>

You will notice from the example above that I've used only two primary meta tags. These tags include the *Title* tag and the *Description* tag. Many SEO's have stopped using the keyword tag and for good reason. It's believed that Google doesn't even consider the keyword tag anymore so there's no harm in simply leaving it blank. More meta tags exist but the title tag and description tag are the most important ones you'll need to use when thinking about improving your ranking in search engine results pages (SERPs). Other tags like the "robots" tag and "author" tags are helpful, but they aren't crucial to getting you ranked on top. Let's discuss each of the before mentioned tags separately and make sure you understand how to create each individual tag.

Did you know?

Depending on your website platform, accessing your meta tags can be really easy. Check for a plugin like Yoast or page editor that gives you direct access to your web page code.

Title

This tag is the page title. Not only does it tell search engines what the main theme of your page is, it also shows up as the title of your website on a search engine results page. For example, using the title I noted for my own website, "Big Fin SEO | Affordable Search Engine Optimization", users will see this exact text when they google my company name. This is the beauty of SEO, you can control how your pages show up in search results. If I wanted the title to be different I could quickly change the meta title on my site's home page and it would be reflected in Google search results.

As a general rule of thumb, make sure your title tag is *no more than seven words and less than sixty characters*, including spaces. This is the maximum number of letters and spaces displayed as a Google title. If your title is longer, it could run off and include three trailing dots when appearing in Google search results. On mobile, the length is even shorter (about 40 characters) but will wrap to the next line.

The reason you want to limit your title tag to only seven words is because Google places a weight (level of importance) on each word in your title tag. Therefore, the more words you have, the less weight applied to each word. This is why it's so important that your title tag contains the key theme of your web page or website and focuses on your keywords.

Note: Place your keywords in the title tag! I'll be covering keywords in the next section, so for the time being just remember that your title tag should include your keywords. Also, don't be afraid to lead with your non-branded keywords on top level pages of your website. Your site should naturally rank well for your brand name so putting it at the end of your title tag is perfectly acceptable. On lower level pages of your website, including your company name is not necessary.

Update: It used to be common to focus on two keyword phrases in your title tag and separate with a post (example: Internet Marketing Expert | Marketing Secrets). However, Google is no longer providing benefit to webmasters using multiple keyword phrases in their page titles. Due to a variety of updates, Google has become much more advanced and interested in the context of the title tag in relation to a user's search and page content. If you see other sites using multiple keyword phrases in their title tags, they're probably missing out on ranking opportunities and applying outdated optimization techniques. Don't dilute your keyword strength unnecessarily.

As a final note, work within the framework provided for title tag creation. By using up to seven words in your tag, you can develop many keyword combinations, mixing and matching terms. Keep in mind that every title tag you place should be unique but related. Using the same title tag on multiple pages can negatively impact your ranking.

Description

This tag provides a description of your website or web page. When you enter a description for your web page it will show up under the website title in the Google search engine results listing. Meta descriptions can be any length, but Google generally truncates snippets to around 155–160 characters. It's best to keep meta descriptions long enough that they're sufficiently descriptive, so keep descriptions as close to 160 characters as possible.

I like to use my keywords in the description tag twice if possible— yes, two times. This has a direct impact on my SERPs and helps to improve click-through rates. The impact to Google is minimal but does help with your overall optimization efforts and click through rate as search terms are highlighted on search results. If you can, work your keywords into a description that seems natural and be sure to repeat your keyword phrase. Your description should be compelling and accurately describe what users will find when they click through to your page. This consistency is important to Google and the user experience.

Example of what to do:

> "*SEO Made Simple* can help you improve **Google search results**. Read testimonials of those who have improved their **Google search results** with these secrets."

Example of what NOT to do:

> "**Google search results**, **Google search results**, improve **Google search results**, buy this book to improve **Google search results**."

Overemphasizing your keyword phrase and stuffing your web page description can have a negative impact on your search engine rankings. Try to use your keyword phrase twice and no more. And be sure to generate a descriptive tag that compels browsers to click through to your website. This can provide a significant increase in the number of browsers who actually click through to your site from the search engine results page. Google has confessed that click-through rate is a significant driver of rankings.

Keywords

The keywords tag is another way to educate search engines about your website but is no longer necessary. This is due to Google's algorithm being able to determine the context of your webpage or digital asset based on other criteria. My belief is that keywords themselves don't carry significant weight in isolation, but analyzed in conjunction with the overall theme of your page, could signal Google as to the legitimacy of your content.

The keyword tag, if used, should include your main keywords, those you've chosen as the main focus of your website, as well as those associated with the theme of your web page. That being said, as long as you follow the other on-page techniques explained in this book, there's no need to use the keyword meta tag.

Note: *Avoid keyword stuffing.* When users place keywords on their web page or within their meta tags over and over again in an effort to improve SERPs—search engines (like Google) actually discredit the value of the web page.

When including keywords on your actual web page, you may want to think about keyword density and placement. Keyword density is the frequency of your keyword phrase in relation to all the words appearing on your web page. Although some SEOs still debate the value of keyword density, I find positive results when keyword density is between 2 and 4 percent. Meaning, only use your keyword phrase 1 – 3 times for every 500 words that appear on the page. Google is smart enough to know what your page is about... so you don't have to go out of your way to tell it.

That being said, it's important to make sure you're using other words that reflect the topic your page is about. For example, if you're focused on teaching people how to build a bird house, you may only use "bird house" a few times but you better include things like "birds", "wood", and "glue". With just a few related phrases, images, etc. Google will know exactly what your page is about and what to rank it for in search results.

Author

A Meta Author tag declares the author of the HTML or XML document of a website. An example of a Meta Author tag is as follows:

<meta name="Author" content="Michael Fleischner ">

In the Meta Author tag it will reference the name of the person who created the HTML or XML document for the site being viewed. If you use the Meta Author tag, it is recommended that you use the author's first and last names to avoid any conflict with other authors who share the same name.

The Meta Author tag is optional to use for your website but we know that Google is using this tag to pass authority to specific content, influencing it's ranking in search results. If you have many individuals that are contributing to the content of your website, use the Meta Author tag to help track the author who wrote specific pages.

Personally, I like to use this tag to track the individual in my company that authored the page and let Google know that someone from my company is the originator of the content. This is particularly handy when other sites have copied our website pages and neglected to take out the Meta Author tag. It's always great to hear their denials of plagiarism but even more important is the fact that Google credits our site with original content.

Robots

The simplest of all meta tags, the robots tag, signals the Googlebot, Google's search engine spider, to crawl your entire website. In order to index your website properly and include all of your web pages, search engines send their spiders to review and scan your website on a regular basis. Google does this every two or three days. Some argue that the robots tag is no longer necessary for a full crawl.

Whether true or not, this is something I don't leave to chance. Adding the robots tag and uploading a sitemap to Google webmaster tools is the best way I know to help Google find all of the content on your website.

When the crawlers view your meta tags and see that your robots tag indicates "all," they simply start crawling. Although some spiders would search the majority of your site without the tag, having it provides the added direction to search engine crawlers. Make sure the robots tag is included in your meta tags to improve crawling rates.

There are some Internet marketers or webmasters who recommend submitting each page of your site directly to search engines via single page submission. I don't think this is even possible anymore and even if it were, it isn't necessary, especially if you're including the robots tag. Search engine crawlers do all the work for you.

What's important is that Google indexes your site, and when it does, it can find all of your content. The robots tag can help with that process. Equally, if not more important, is compliance with W3C standards (industry accepted HTML standards) and a sitemap. When you combine the robots tag with an easily indexed website, Google and other search engines can find and index all of the pages on your website or blog.

URLs

Many people believe that if you have a special URL, one that contains the keyword you're trying to rank highly for, you'll be number one on Google. **This isn't true but it helps.** The reality is that having your keyword in your URL does help in many instances but is not essential. In fact, past Google updates, exact match domains (domains consisting of only your target keyword phrase) were targeted– penalizing them for trying to game the system. Exact match domain penalties only impacted about 3% of active domains but underscores the fact that having a keyword as your entire domain name (URL) isn't enough for number one rankings.

Let's explore this idea a little further. If this URL theory were correct, then a site that wanted to rank well for "seo company" could simply buy the URL of www.seocompany.com. But do a search on Google for "seo company" and see what happens. You'll discover that seocompany.com doesn't even rank on the first page. This is because there are hundreds of factors that weigh in to number one rankings and exact match domains are no longer a sure thing. I do believe that having a portion of your keyword phrase in the URL is helpful (i.e. SEO.com shows in results).

Having your keyword phrase in the URL also helps with local search. Although probably not as important as including "SEO" in a title tag or having a site full of search engine optimization related content, having your keyword – in this example "SEO", in the URL can certainly help point to your site's theme. A more important factor is URL length. According to a recent Ahrefs study of over 2 million URLs, shorter URL's performed better in search results.

In addition to having your keyword in your own URLs, you can also have your keywords in URLs that point to your website. Referred to as 'link building', having keyword rich anchor text is an essential link building strategy. Each time a website links to your website using only your URL address (example: http://www.seocompany.com), if that URL is partially made up of keywords, it provides a boost to Google search results. As I'll show you later, having the right link profile, including your URL, variations of the URL, brand name, and target keywords, can help boost search engine results significantly.

Another great example of this URL concept is the keyword phrase "gopher." Go to Google and enter the search term, "gopher." If the URL theory was correct—that you have to own the URL that contains only your keywords—you would expect the first search result to be www.gopher.com. However, the first few results are for authoritative sites like YouTube and Wikipedia.

Why? It's because more sites link to the YouTube videos and Wikipedia's listing of "gopher" and it has more authority than the next authoritative sites listed. As I mentioned, there are a lot of factors that go into producing top rankings and having the perfect URL is just one of them.

Another technique that I have found to be particularly useful from an SEO perspective is buying aged domains. An aged domain is one that was established some time ago and may even have some traffic coming to it. You can search for and buy aged domains using GoDaddy or Sedo.com. If you can purchase an aged domain that already has a portion of your primary keyword phrase included, the better. This can give you a jump start when launching your website because it has been indexed by Google, likely has inbound links, and may currently rank for the keywords for which you're trying to optimize.

HTTPS://

Before we leave the topic of URLs, it's important to talk about SSL certificates. When you browse a website, its address either starts with http: or https: The second one, https://, means the site is secure. Some time ago, Google began penalizing sites that do not have the https:// designation, which means your site has acquired an SSL certificate. SSL stand for Secure Socket Layer.

An SSL is the backbone of a secure Internet and it protects your sensitive information as it travels across the world's computer networks. SSL is essential for protecting your website, even if it doesn't handle sensitive information like credit cards. Getting an SSL is rather easy to do and provided by most hosting companies.

If your website does not have an SSL certificate, get one now. You can confirm whether or not you have one by typing in https:// followed by your website URL. If your site doesn't appear with the https:// designation, you don't have an active SSL certificate. Sites with an SSL certificate should redirect to https: when users type in any version of their site - http://, www., etc. Check with your hosting provider and make the small investment in an SSL certificate if you want to improve website rankings.

Clean Code (W3C Validation)

As mentioned previously, I'm not a programmer, and, in fact, I know very little about web development. But I do know there is a right way and a wrong way to design a website. How do I know? I learned my lesson the hard way—through trial and error. Once I made the appropriate changes designed to help my SEO, my SERPs began to climb. That's how I discovered the importance of proper formatting and coding.

If you work for a company or have ever made a call to a customer support representative, you know that businesses operate according to specific standards and service levels. The same is true when it comes to web programming. When dealing with website code, these standards are referred to as W3C. The acronym W3C stands for the World Wide Web Consortium. You can learn more about the consortium by visiting their website at http://www.w3c.org.

For implementation of proper SEO techniques, you should verify that your website meets these industry standards. In my opinion WC3 has become a bit outdated, but there's a good chance that Google is still using them. When visiting the W3C website you can learn more about W3C and even check to see if your site code meets W3C standards by using their free validation tool at http://validator.w3.org/. I recommend using this free tool that provides specific feedback as to which area(s) of your code meet HTML standards and which do not. Run each key page of your website through the validator.

Any errors you encounter will need to be fixed by someone who knows the code in which your website was written. It is important for you to resolve the coding errors noted for a variety of reasons—not the least of which is that Google will have an even easier time evaluating your website. If using Wordpress, search for W3C plugins that can identify or remedy any coding issues.

Note: Be sure to use cascading style sheets (CSS) when developing your website pages. A Cascading Style Sheet (CSS) is a file containing code that dictates the look and formatting of a web page. This helps to keep your code very clean. Instead of placing formatting code on the page itself, make a call to your CSS, which allows you to reference all of the design-related elements you need across your website. Don't be too concerned if you're not familiar with cascading style sheets. Anyone who works in the area of web design has used them and can provide guidance when designing your site. Most template sites already do this for you.

Heading Tags (<h1>, <h2>, and <h3>)

Heading tags (sometimes referred to as *headers*) are used to emphasize text on a web page. Search engines love to see these header tags because pages with large headings indicate the substance and importance of the content. Use the tag—either <h1>, <h2>, or <h3>—that's appropriate for your page and be sure to include your keywords in the tag. For example: <h1>free marketing articles</h1>.

Using the <h1> tag will display your text in a rather large format unless altered via CSS. The <h2> tag displays text slightly smaller than an <h1>. The <h3> tag displays text smaller than <h2> and so on. Try to use at least one <h1> tag on the page you are trying to optimize.

Don't overdo it on your heading tags. One to three is sufficient on a page. The key is to make it flow well and appear natural. Placing tags that make your text appear unnatural will only hurt your website's readability and performance. Google sees that you're emphasizing text using these tags and giving the phrase a stronger weight.

Alt Image Tags

Do you use graphics or images on your website? If you do, each image should contain an alt tag. An alt tag is simply the practice of naming a photo, image, or icon. You can check to see if your website images already have alt tags associated with them by running your mouse over the image. If an alt tag is in place, text should display. If text does not display, an alt tag is not present and needs to be added.

The literal benefit of an alt tag is that the text displays while your website images are loading, giving users information about the content included on your page. The primary purpose for alt text is to ensure people with disabilities can read the page. The secondary benefit (or primary SEO benefit) is that Google takes these keyword phrases into account when evaluating your website content.

The best way to tag your images is with your keyword phrase followed by additional content. For multiple images, use slightly different wording. For example, if you're selling widgets and optimizing for *discount widgets*, you would include an <alt> image tag for your widget using the alt text *"discount widgets on sale"*.

The code that would be used to insert an image tag in this example:

```
<img src="../images/widgets1.jpg" width="125" height="60"
border="0" alt="discount widgets on sale">
```

As with any optimization effort, don't overdo it with images or alt tags. Too many images can result in a slow loading website, negatively impacting site load speed. Images that contain too many tags can signal keyword stuffing. Don't neglect using alt tags for every image on your page. Be sure to label them with a single keyword phrase.

The last thing I'd like you to keep in mind relates to images in general. Keep in mind that part of your website success depends on visitors staying and interacting with your content. In addition to tagging your images properly, it's important to choose the right images. Use royalty free photos from sites like Pexels to offer high definition photos that engage your users.

Proper Keyword Placement

You must focus on where and how your keywords are placed on your web page. The frequency of placement is less important than once considered as we mentioned previously as Google has gotten more sophisticated with their ability to identify what your content is about based on just a few related keyword phrases.

Many people believe that if they fill their web pages with nothing but keywords, they can get top placement. Search engines have responded to this and actually penalize sites that over use keywords. The number of times your keyword appears on a given web page is called keyword density and you don't need much of it.

The concept of keyword density isn't talked about much anymore but is important to understand as well as the location of your keywords. The number of times your keywords are used on a given page as a percentage of the total number of words is a great start but doesn't give us everything we need to fully optimize a given webpage. For reference, I like keyword density of 2 to 3 percent but never more than 4 percent.

Of greater importance is the placement and treatment of your keywords. Use the following guidelines to optimize your page:

- Place your keyword(s) in the title tag, description tag, and alt tags.
- Place keyword(s) in an <h1>, <h2>, and/or <h3> tag.
- Place keyword(s) in the first twenty-five words of your page.
- Once in the body of your page, and
- Place your keyword(s) in the last twenty-five words of your page.

Note: A great way to get keywords in the last twenty-five words is by adding it to your page footer after the copyright. For example, "© Your Site Name. Your Site Keyword." Adding your keyword phrase in this fashion is relatively natural and appears virtually unnoticed to those using your site.

Following these guidelines for proper keyword placement shows Google that your keywords are important to your web page and your website. It also helps you compete with other sites that are not as well optimized using these on-page factors.

The reason I take keyword placement seriously is because we don't know how much of your page the Google bot is crawling. Of course the assumption is everything top to bottom, but do we know for certain? The answer is no, so we need to cover the basis. Based on some work we've done recently, pages that included keywords in the body section of the page performed much better than including a keyword phrase in the sidebar or footer.

No Flash and JavaScript External

In addition to ensuring that your website code is up to standards, avoid Flash and JavaScript on your page. In my entire career, I have *never* seen a site that leads with a Flash intro rank number one on Google. If you can find one, I'd be surprised.

Flash intros do not provide keyword content in a manner that is easily searchable by Google. Even if the Flash intro was well developed and contained your keywords in some shape or form, the Google spider would not be able to read it. The whole idea of a Flash demo, which is a self-contained entity consisting of dense code is the exact opposite of what Google values. Google searches for open content that is readable and easily navigated.

Is all Flash bad? Only if your site is completely Flash based or your homepage consists of nothing more than a Flash presentation. If your intro page is largely Flash or contains flash sliders with little room for additional text on the page, I encourage you to replace it with an HTML focused homepage. If Flash is still important, provide a link to your Flash script from your homepage. Also, consider using built in sliders like Slider Revolution if you're using WordPress. By doing so, you can optimize your homepage and then drive users to view your Flash demo.

JavaScript, a type of code often used for the creation of buttons, navigation, tracking, and so on, is another double-edged sword. Using JavaScript can improve a user's experience but at the same time, it can have a detrimental effect on your SERPs.

My recommendation is that if you would like to use JavaScript, place the code in an external file. This removes the majority of JavaScript code that appears on your site, helping your webpage load faster, and brings your most important content (meta tags, etc.) closer to the top of your page. You could also use a website plugin if you're on Wordpress, to minimize Java script code.

Sitemaps

A sitemap is a single page on your website that provides access to all other pages on your site, at least the most important ones. Sitemaps serve an important purpose. They enable search engines to spider your site much quicker. I strongly believe they are helpful in the optimization game – especially XML sitemaps uploaded to Google Search Console.

When a search engine bot arrives at your website, it will read the first page of your site and then start looking at your navigational links which include a link to your sitemap. When the search engine crawler reaches your sitemap, it begins visiting and indexing each link you have listed.

It's a good idea to have more than an index of links on your HTML sitemap. Try to include short paragraphs of descriptive text for each link, which of course should contain your keywords.

You can create your sitemap in HTML. Doing so is easy and only requires an HTML editor. Your sitemap should consist of a single web page with links to your top-level pages.

Some search engines like Google require an XML based sitemap for proper indexing. Creating an XML based sitemap isn't difficult at all. In fact, Google has made it easy for you with more free tools. You can get started with Google sitemaps and other tools by visiting Google at https://search.google.com/search-console.

A number of free programs on the web such as http://www.xml-sitemaps.com can help you create an XML sitemap. Once you've created a XML sitemap that lists all of the pages on your website, upload it to your server and submit it to Google Sitemaps through the *Google Search Console* feature.

Note: Don't forget to update your sitemap every few months or so if you're actively adding content to your website. And you should be. We'll discuss content later in this guide so for now just keep in mind that as your site changes, and so should your sitemap to reflect all of the changes you've made.

Uploading your sitemap to Google can have a positive impact on SERPs. Take the time to learn more about sitemaps, develop, and publish your own sitemap in html and xml.

Internal Linking

One of the most important on-page optimization opportunities you have is to develop a simple and direct internal linking strategy. Internal linking refers to the linking structure your site uses to reach secondary pages on your website – pages that are lower down in the hierarchy. How you link from one page to another is very important but often overlooked or dismissed as a minimal strategy. The reality is that many sites can significantly improve their rankings based on a strong internal linking strategy.

Internal linking provides direct access to your web pages in order of importance. The best practice for internal linking is to link to your main category pages from your website's homepage. To illustrate, let's say that I've created a website related to clothing.

In this example, the website's homepage is all about clothing and the types of clothing being offered for sale. From the home page you can access main category pages related to specific types of clothing. For example, "men's clothing", "women's clothing", "kid", etc. Once users navigate from the homepage to a given category they can drill down even further to see, "shirts", "pants", and so on. Within these areas of focus you can read all about products, prices, and how to order individual items. To facilitate easy navigation, the homepage has links to each of the category pages.

Category pages may also be referred to as "top-level pages." The reason I use this label is because each of these pages is directly accessible from the home page in just one click. There are numerous benefits to this type of architecture which I'll be covering in more detail but essentially, the closer a webpage is to your root domain (www.sample.com), the more page authority it will possess. Domain Authority (DA) and Page Authority (PA) are directly correlated with website rankings. These measures refer to the overall importance of your website – domain or page. This has been proven over and over again when analyzing top ranked web pages. Keep your navigation simple and focus on a top down structure that passes authority to your most important web pages first and foremost.

Although internal linking can be accomplished in a variety of ways, this is just one example of a basic linking structure you can follow. Here are some tips you can use to ensure your internal linking is designed properly:

- Include links to all of your main category pages from your homepage by placing links in a navigation menu. This menu should be available on each page of your website. Also, you can place links to your category pages in your website footer.

- Include your keywords in links where possible. This tells Google what content can be found on the other side of the link and reinforces your internal linking strategy.

- Don't place more than three links to the same page on your homepage. This is unnecessary and it could trigger potential issues with the Google search engine.

- Remember that your page is hierarchical, meaning that your home page and top level pages have the most authority. Pass that authority to the pages that matter most on your websites.

Never underestimate the power of internal linking. Internal links are important because they allow for easy access to your content by search engine crawlers and can transfer authority between web pages.

Warning: Make sure your internal, and external links, aren't broken. There's nothing more frustrating to a user than clicking on a link that goes nowhere or gives them a 404 error. This is true for site links as well as those pointing to a third party site. Moreover, Google penalizes sites with too many broken links. Top ranking website have less than 2% broken links. Use a link checker to make sure you're okay. Search Google for a broken link finder and run a check, fixing any broken links on your site.

This wraps up some of the most important on-page optimization factors you should be working with to improve website rankings. From meta tags to title tags and even internal linking, on page optimization is essential for top rankings. Remember, an on-page optimization effort can't be effective without considering what keyword phrases you are optimizing your web pages for and integrating them into your site. Always have 1-2 target keyword phrases that you're focused on integrating into each web page. Trying to optimize for more than one or two per page will hinder your efforts for top rankings.

Final Three

On page optimization is comprised of a number of factors as we've already discussed. And keyword usage is where on page optimization begins to blend with off page optimization. But it all begins with a well-designed, fully optimized website. As I've mentioned throughout this guide, making sure that your technical (on-page) SEO is taken care of is the most important beginning to a powerful, well ranking site. I'd also like to stress three important factors to consider before we start talking about off-page optimization. These areas have only grown in importance as Google's algorithm has evolved to improve the overall search experience.

Factor 1: Engaging Content. Google is really focused on evaluating the usefulness of content. There are a variety of ways this can be identified including time on page, number of views, and most importantly the number of shares. In fact, with a closer correlation between social media, time on site, and click-through-rates, greater focus should be placed on developing engaging content.

This is one of the reasons why long-form content still works well. It keeps users on a web page longer and encourages sharing. If you haven't already integrated social sharing icons into specific content pages of your website, now would be a good time to do so. As your content gets shared, it builds authority through inbound links and popularity.

When producing content for your website and webpages, focus your effort on original, engaging content. I like to think about "long-form" content as integral to any SEO effort that builds authority and produces strong search results. Long form content is anywhere from 800 – 1,600 words and uses sub-heads, bullets, images, and even a topical index, to make navigation easy on both mobile and desktop. As noted earlier, include "Share" buttons on your webpages to help engagement scores.

If you're trying to rank for position zero, appearing at the top of search results, consider doing your research before authoring your content. Although long form content that's easily navigable is a must, you can learn from what others are doing who are currently in the top spot. Often times, with just a little bit of research, we can see someone appearing in the top result for our target keyword with outdated or incomplete content. If you model their content strategy and framework, you can often achieve a similar result give the right inbound link profile and page authority.

Factor 2: Website Load Speed. A fast loading website is a very important ranking factor, it always has been. By using Google Mobile Speed Test or some other type of free online tool like GTmetrix to help determine how fast your website loads, compared to your competition, is an important step in the ranking process. Faster loading websites generally do better in search engine result listings (SERPs). This is because Google is interested in improving the online experience for users. If you clicked on a search result and did nothing but wait you'd grow impatient with Google and move on to the next search engine. Don't overlook the importance of a fast loading website! Since the mobile first update website load speed has only become more important to your rankings.

Keep in mind that you want your site to perform well on both desktop and mobile. However, Google is indexing mobile first making it the best place to start. One way to test your load speed is with the Google Mobile Speed Test. Based on the analysis, you can update your site to respond more quickly. This will give you site an edge when it comes the competition.

Factor 3: Google Analytics. Tracking how people interact with your website calls for additional focus here, whether you like data or not. When you know and understand how people arrive at your site, how they navigate, stay, interact, and leave your site, you can dramatically improve engagement and popularity which are helpful from an SEO perspective. Engagement is when someone comes to your website and clicks on, or navigates to, specific content. For example, you may find that most of your visitors to your organically because of a blog post you did about a on topic. This would be an indication of what people want and you could replicate it with additional blog posts.

The opposite is also true. When you have the proper tracking code on your site, Google Analytics or some other type of web based tracking, you can see where people are leaving. Most websites have a 50% or higher abandonment rate on their home page. People get there and go back out to search results without clicking further. But some of your content might be really sticky. That's what you want to learn so you can avoid this type of content in the future.

By considering and implementing all of the on-page factors associated with a well optimized site, you can gain an advantage against other websites competing for your select group of keywords. Start with effective keyword research and turn your attention to building or maintaining a well optimized website using the techniques we shared.

Section One Summary

Here's what you should take away from this section about on-page optimization:

- ✓ On-page optimization is what you do on your website to influence SERPs on Google.

- ✓ Doing proper keyword research is the first step to a successful SEO campaign.

- ✓ Keyword development is one of the most important on-page optimization strategies.

- ✓ Research keywords and competing websites to select ideal keywords.

- ✓ Research the strength of competing websites before selecting your final keywords using Google PR and authority (ex: number of inbound links).

- ✓ Having proper meta tags is essential. Always include your keyword phrase(s) in your meta tags.

- ✓ The proper meta tags include your title tag, description tag, keywords tag, and robots tag.

- ✓ Choose your URL carefully. Your URL doesn't have to have your keyword included but it helps when other sites link to your site. Avoid exact match domains.

- ✓ How you format your page is important for optimization purposes.

- ✓ Make sure you design your web pages so Google is forced to read your on-page content first.

- ✓ Verify that your code is W3C compliant.

- ✓ Don't forget to include your keyword phrase(s) in <h1>, <h2>, and <h3> header tags. This signifies the importance of your content to Google.

✓ Label each graphic with an alt tag that includes your keyword phrase.

✓ Eliminate Flash if it's the main presentation of your website. Google does not view this favorably.

✓ If you're going to use JavaScript to enhance the overall visitor experience of your website, place the code in an external file.

✓ Include a sitemap that's easily accessible by Google. Submit an XML version of your sitemap through Google Webmaster Tools.

✓ Never underestimate the power of internal linking. A good internal linking structure can improve your SERPs.

✓ Developing engaging content is one of the most important things you can do to optimize your website. Make it easy to share pages on social media.

✓ Page load speed is a significant factor in Google rankings. Ensure that your home page loads more quickly than those of competing sites.

✓ Track what's happening on your website and learn how to improve engagement.

Section 2

Off-Page Optimization

Off-Page Optimization

As I mentioned in the introduction, there are essentially two parts to any SEO effort once you've completed your keyword research: *on-page optimization* and *off-page optimization*. Off-page optimization is just as important as on page optimization and in fact may be a more powerful factor when it comes to increasing your search engine results on Google. In my experience, about 60 percent or more of your results are directly correlated to off-page optimization.

In fact, after years of consulting for large companies, I've proven in some instances that it's possible to achieve positive results without actually applying on-page optimization if using off-page techniques properly. However, going down the path of skipping on-page optimization is a difficult one and no longer an option when trying to achieve top rankings. Always begin your SEO campaign with on-page optimization to build a powerful foundation.

Now that we've discussed the importance of starting with on-page optimization, it's time to focus on the next step of any effective search engine campaign—off-page optimization.

What Is Off-Page Optimization?

In its simplest form, off-page optimization can be referred to as increasing a website's authority. This authority is defined by the number and types of websites that link to a given website or URL. I also like to think of off-page optimization as what you do on the Internet, *not directly on your website*, to improve search engine result placements.

The best part of off-page optimization is that there are a handful of proven techniques you can start using today to improve your SERPs on the world's largest search engine.

Off-page optimization is one of the most important SEO strategies for those seeking number one placement on Google. The fastest and most effective way to achieve this goal is by developing quality links to your website. When I refer to "quality," I'm referring to links from sites that:

- Have an equivalent or higher Google authority than your site

- Include similar content to your web page

- Use related meta tags

- Come from diverse sources

- Have been around for a while, i.e. age

- Have a large number of quality sites linking to them

Even more important than the *what* (quality websites) is the *how*. Specifically, how these quality websites link to you is an essential key to Google dominance.

Did you know?

Your success on Google is DIRECTLY correlated to how well you implement off-page optimization—the types of websites that link to you and how they are linking to you.

This is the biggest secret to Google dominance – especially over the long-term. Using this "secret" has changed my failure into success. Let me give you some examples to reinforce the point.

Let's explore the importance of inbound links, links that point to your website, using a little more context. Assuming that all on page factors are equal, which they never are, the site that has more quality inbound links will rank higher than the site that has fewer inbound links. It's important to note that we never know which factors Google is weighing more heavily, on-page or off-page, but we do know that both matter and that inbound links are an essential part of off-page optimization.

This can often be seen when we do a search and find a top ranked website that has many more inbound links compared to the 2nd or 3rd result. Conversely, there will be situations where the number one ranked website doesn't have a ton of inbound links but their on-page optimization is on-point. This is why researching your competition is so important and why tools like SEMrush, Moz, etc. are so vital to begin using. They provide insights into why certain sites or page rank the way they do.

Even though Google is all about mobile first, natural language, etc. I still see sites in position zero, or position one, that are not as authoritative as those in position 2 -10. A good example of this is "Free marketing articles". If you Google that phrase you'll notice a very outdated site on top of search results. This is probably due to the age of the domain and the focus on marketing articles. Google clearly views this as being the closest match to my query, so that's the results that comes out on top. In this case, inbound links are still important but it looks like on page factors are being weighted heavily as well. The reality is you can't do one without the other. That's why it's important to understand the anatomy of an inbound link and how to use them to your advantage.

As I've already mentioned, having more inbound links alone will not give you a higher ranking. Based on years in this industry and working with over a 1,000 clients, I can tell you that it's not just a numbers game. It goes well beyond quantity. Google caught on to link farms and other attempts to game the system years ago. Yes, you need as many inbound links as you can get but only if they have value.

Your rankings have more to do with link quality than anything else. Although link quality can be difficult to define because there are so many parameters to consider, some basic ones include link age, anchor text, and site authority. You also need to consider where the link is coming from. Is another site linking to you from their home page often referred to as a top level domain (TLD) or some obscure page very low down in their hierarchy? As we've already covered, pages that are far from the root domain have very little authority. If that's the case, then linking to you doesn't pass much if any authority to your website.

The other area to consider is that of anchor text, the text users see and click on to visit the URL destination. Google has made a very big deal of this concept which essentially tries to weed out all of the SEO's who are intentionally trying to optimize for a specific keyword. For example, if all the sites linking to your page said, "this is the best product ever" instead of "http://www.samplesite.com", "samplesite.com", "top 10 products…", or "click here", their search engine value to Google would be diminished. What I'm trying to say is that you need some diversity in your link anchor text. That's because if 100 out of 100 inbound links all use the same anchor text, Google would see this as unnatural, a deliberate attempt to game off-page optimization factors. This is why it's important to stress how external links are designed when pointing to your website so they appear natural, creating a normal link profile (more on proper link building strategies and techniques in the section: 'How to Link').

Achieving top rankings for your website is based on a combination of on-page factors and off-page factors including the quality of inbound links, link authority, and link text. By keeping this in mind when considering link structure, you can make sure that any inbound link you receive provides SEO benefit. If you set down the road of link building without the proper framework, inbound links may not pass all the value you're hoping for.

Link Types

Before going any further, let me go deeper on linking by explaining various link types. This is essential to understand if you want to master off-page optimization through link building. There really are only three types of links you need to know about: *one-way links*, *reciprocal links*, and *three-way links*.

- **One-way links.** These are links from a website that is not your own. Also referred to as third-party websites, these sites place a link from one or more of their web pages to your website or digital asset (blog, landing page, etc.).

  Google values one-way links above all else. One-way links are incredibly powerful, if they're quality links, because you are receiving a vote from an independent third party.

- **Reciprocal links.** When you exchange links with another website, commonly referred to as *swapping links*, you're providing a link to their site, from your own, in exchange for a link from their website to yours. Reciprocal links have some value, but are much less valuable than one-way links.

- **Three-way links.** Three-way linking is when you partner with another website (site B) and provide a link from your site (site A) to their site. In turn, they provide a link from another site they own (site C) back to your site. Essentially a one-way link.

I'm often asked about outbound links in addition to in-bound links. An out bound link would be a link from your website to someone else's site or an authority website like a social media account or reference site. Google has said that outbound links do not necessarily help you, but they certainly don't hurt either. That is, unless linking out to a shady website. Make sure outbound links are to authority websites only and related to your site content.

How to Get Links To Your Website?

Now that you know the importance of links, the first question you must ask yourself is how to get other websites linking to yours? There are a variety of strategies to apply here for attracting quality one-way links. Regardless of which strategy you choose, begin with a mindset of attracting quality links! The goal should always be to produce something of such value that other sites are pointing their respective audiences to your specific content, webpage or website. This is what's been driving the content marketing revolution and for good reason. "Getting links" is not as easy as it used to be, so earning them has become the name of the game. There are entire books and websites dedicated to developing a content marketing strategy that works, so I won't attempt to explain it here, but know that effective link development begins with quality content that others want to share by linking to your website, social media, and blogs. When focusing on local SEO, there are some specialized link building strategies that we'll cover in a later section.

If you build it they will come. While you're producing content and pushing it out through social media channels, you should simultaneously take a proactive approach to build quality inbound links to your site content. If you work this strategy in conjunction with your content development efforts, there are a few shortcuts that can save time and help you get quality link placements.

Getting links starts with knowing which links to get. Before you move ahead begging and pleading for just anyone to link to your site, first decide who you want links from.

The most effective way to identify the "right" sites to get links from should be based on who is linking to your competition, which is defined by who outranks you on Google for your target keyword. This is a very important strategy and one that is frequently overlooked for achieving top rankings. Simply stated, you should be evaluating who links to the number one search result in Google for your target keyword phrase and try to acquire links from the same websites. I know it sounds obvious but very few sites use this basic strategy for developing their link program.

Did you know?

If you get the same sites to link to your site using a natural link profile, and you've optimized your site well, in time you will outrank your competition on Google for the same keyword phrases.

Many methods can help you determine which sites are linking to the number one result in Google for the keyword phrase you're targeting. Begin by identifying which site is in the first position for your search term. You can do this by visiting Google and typing in your search term. Record the URL of the number one search result. Once you've identified this site, do one of the following:

- **Google search.** Go to Google.com and type in your target search term. After reviewing the first website search result, type the following text into the Google search bar, *Link: www.nameoftoprankedcompetitor.com*, making sure to replace the targeted phrase "nameoftoprankedcompetitor" with the name of the site you've identified as having the number one position on Google for your search term.

  The result will be a series of sites linking to your competitor. The only downside to this method is that you won't know which sites are more important than others (e.g., the number of links linking into those sites, authority, keyword content on pages, etc.), but it will certainly identify all of the sites you need to target for link-building purposes. It will also reveal the internal links that are giving the site some ranking authority.

- **Online SEO tools.** I have found that using online marketing tools to automatically generate a list of sites linking into your competitor's website, as well as link details such as Google PR, link text, page title, and so on, can be the most effective way to generate a list of targeted sites for your link-development efforts.

  I've personally bought and used about a dozen different products to help me keep an eye on my competition and, more importantly build an effective linking campaign. I regularly use SEO software because in less than thirty seconds, I know exactly which sites are linking to the number one positioned website for my target phrase and receive information that helps me prioritize my efforts like the Page Rank of each inbound link and domain age. As I mentioned previously, I prefer SEMrush, Moz, or a plugin. You can often accomplish the same outcome without purchasing SEO software. However, these tools save you a significant amount of effort, reducing the time required for acquiring in-depth link-building information.

You can use whatever SEO or link analysis software you want as long as it provides you a list of sites linking into your competitors and a way to prioritize that list. If you start to develop links from the highest quality sites first, your climb to the number one spot on Google will happen that much faster.

- **Identify authority websites**. Authority websites are those sites linking to three or more of your competitors. If you don't have a SEO tool at your disposal, you can accomplish this manually using the following method:

    1. Search for competitive sites by visiting Google and searching for your most important search term.

    2. Create or download a spreadsheet of the top one hundred sites "linking in" to each of your top five competitors (Microsoft Excel is a good tool for this).

    3. Sort by authority.

    4. While looking at the list see if any of the website URLs are duplicated across your list or use the "find" function. If the site appears two or more times, highlight it.

    5. Once you've developed your list of authoritative sites, visit each one to determine how your competitors are listed and how you can acquire a link to your website.

Model the strategy your competitors have used. If these sites are directories, look for a directory submission form. If the links are from articles that your competitors submitted, submit your own. If all you can locate is an e-mail, ask the webmaster to include a link to your site. You may also suggest a link exchange if the opportunity arises.

If the website is already linking to your competition, they are a prime target for a link exchange or for adding your link because they see value in linking to sites covering similar subject matter.

The fastest way to achieve top rankings is to try to get links from the same sites that are linking to the number one, two, and three top search results for your desired keyword. You won't be able to get links from all of them and, in fact, may only be able to get a few, but each inbound link can benefit you.

After applying the competitive link strategy, the next step is to build quality inbound links to your website through a natural link profile. Before I cover specific strategies for acquiring links, you must first understand the proper way to format an inbound link and achieve a natural link profile for maximum results.

How to Link

Now that you know how to find the sites you want to receive links from, you need to learn the proper way to develop a Google-friendly link. Google-friendly links are links that improve the search engine results of a given website. This is one of the ways that I've been able to get much better rankings for my web pages even though I may have fewer links pointing to my site compared to competitors.

I always cover the formatting aspect of linking in detail because your links are virtually worthless if they're not displayed correctly on other websites. Let's begin with the anatomy of a link; for example, let's take a look at http://bigfinseo.com.

As an individual browsing the web, you would likely look at this link, know it was a link, and click on it if relevant to your search. This common application of link design is pervasive throughout the web and used consistently (blue and/or underlined). Another way to present the same link is with alternate link text. For example: Affordable SEO

Link text can also be referred to as *anchor text* and is essential for Google optimization. Embedded behind the link text is an active URL. In the example above, if you were on a web page and positioned your mouse over the *Affordable SEO* text, you would discover the URL of https://bigfinseo.com embedded within.

The question I often get is, "If you're trying to get links to your website from other sites, why wouldn't you want them to simply place the URL of your website on their website?" There are a number of important answers to this question. The reason you wouldn't just include a URL is because Google wants to see a **natural link profile,** and having tons of links with the same anchor text is negatively viewed by their most up-to-date algorithm.

Anchor text is vitally important because it passes signals to Google identifying what your content is all about. You want to give Google the right signals so it appears as though third parties, not you, are developing inbound links to your website, blog, or other digital assets. That's why we call it organic search. Google is trying to mirror the process that each of us go through naturally to find relevant content.

Anchor text for the ideal inbound link profile

One of the past Google algorithm updates changed the game when it comes to link building and diversifying anchor text. Although many people in the search engine optimization field had been aware of the importance of diversifying anchor text in the past, the evidence at the time suggested that diversification didn't matter all that much. Although anchor text never really weighed into my optimization process in any significant way, recent Google algorithm updates have required all SEOs to rethink their anchor text strategies.

The good news is that we've learned a lot about how Google uses anchor text to identify link and site quality. Google is now looking for a natural inbound link profile supported by branded anchor text using your brand or site name and non-branded anchor text which uses keyword phrases that describe your product or service. Even Google confirms that a natural linking profile – one that utilizes many forms of anchor text, has an impact on rankings. This is further supported by tests conducted by third party SEO's using a generic link profile, without the benefit of social signals like Facebook or Instagram Likes, generating an increase in rankings.

To begin, let's consider the 4 main anchor types that most commonly define the largest portion of an inbound link profile:

- **Naked URLs** consist of some variation of the actual URL to a website's internal page or, more commonly, the home page. Naked URLs are the strongest signal to Google of a "natural" inbound link profile. In fact, they typically comprise the majority of anchor text distribution in healthy websites, approximately 70%. Examples include: searchenginejournal.com, http://www.searchenginejournal.com, www.searchenginejournal.com, and even searchenginejournal.com.

- **Brand Anchors** are comprised of some variation of the brand name for the destination website. Even small variations such as differences in capitalization are noted by search engines. Examples include Search Engine Journal,

SearchEngineJournal and SEJ, a common abbreviation for this particular website example.

- **Brand-keyword hybrid anchors** are comprised of some variation of the brand name of the destination URL mixed with a relevant exact-match or LSI (latent semantic indexing) keyword. Examples might include *SEO blog, Search Engine Journal, Search Blog, Search Engine Journal, and Search Engine Journal a search blog.*

- **Universal/junk anchors** are comprised of words that could apply to any destination website, or are universal in nature, such as "click here," "visit this website," and "more." They are commonly known as "junk" anchors because, prior to the latest Google update, SEOs and webmasters used to try to avoid these types of anchors since they passed no definitive signals of relevance to the destination website. However, I wouldn't consider them junk anymore! They are definitely a key part of developing a natural link profile for your website.

Most of the variations you'll see through online link building consist of these four types of anchor text. As you move forward with your inbound link building strategy, avoid the urge to rack up keyword-rich links which were pre-BERT update best practices and instead pick one of the four anchor types above. Also, build links to more than just your home page.

This is extremely important as some SEO's suggest that nearly 60% of all inbound links should not be pointing to your home page but rather other pages on your website. In my thinking I'm not quite there yet because intuitively, most other sites, when referencing a third party site, point to their home page not a sub-level page. Personally, I think it's more important that social related links dig down through key website pages. Remember, search engine optimization can be as much art as it is science.

To rank on top for a particular keyword or keyword phrase, you want third-party websites to place your link with the proper anchor text on their website. Top level domain links are best – links from their home page to yours. Make sure your anchor text includes each of the link types mentioned above when it's in your control. If not, you're still better off getting a link from a quality website regardless of the anchor text.

The makeup of inbound links has an impact on your rankings. Getting value from your inbound links is a combination of your anchor text and the weight that's being passed from the sites you are getting links from. In the past, you could focus on specific non-branded anchor text when building inbound links. For example, I used Marketing Expert as my anchor text again and again. When one of the past Google updates started penalizing sites for focused anchor text being used over and over again, my ranking dropped from number one to page 3 overnight. Why? Because it wasn't considered a natural link profile - especially when more than 50% of inbound links to my site used this keyword phrase instead of my brand of naked URL. I've had to modify my link building strategy to be primarily comprised of my domain URL and only slightly versioned for keywords I'm optimizing for. This could again change in the future. That's why it's important to stay on top of the latest Google algorithm updates but also use a diversified inbound link strategy.

Using another example from the section on keyword research and title tags, you can vary your link text by using more than one keyword variation. For example, in addition to including *women's tennis shoes* in anchor text, we can add another keyword phrase like *Nike tennis shoes.* You can even add multiple keyword phrases (example: Womens Tennis Shoes Featuring Nike Tennis Shoes). The corresponding result is that each time you get your link placed on a third-party website, you're actually optimizing for two keyword phrases instead of one! The HTML code you can use to get this effect, if you're not using a WISYWIG editor, is as follows:

<a href="http://www.yoursitename.com" title="womens tennis shoes" target="_blank" rel="dofollow">Womens Tennis Shoes Featuring Nike Tennis Shoes</a>

As always, be sure to replace http://www.yoursitename.com with your own website URL and obviously use the appropriate title including your keyword phrase. I also like my links to open in a separate window (a.k.a. target= "_blank") and be marked as "dofollow". This tells search engine spiders to follow the link back to my site. When engaging in reciprocal link exchanges, three-way link exchanges, or if simply requesting a link from a site, provide them with the link formatting noted above.

Make sure that every time a website links to you they are using the specific linking format you want using anchor text that includes your URL, keyword[s] or keyword phrase[s]. I can't tell you how many times possible link partners have asked me for a link exchange and submitted their link to me without specifying exactly what they wanted for anchor text. Personally I don't like leaving link building to chance if I can avoid it. Make sure links are "do follow". This tells Google that a link placed on a page should be followed to the destination and indexed. If someone is placing a "no follow" link to your website on theirs, it's recognized by Google but doesn't necessarily pass all the authority it could to your webpage. If you're proactively engaging link partners, be transparent about what you'd like to happen. The same is true with regard to the links you're providing in exchange.

Applying proper link formatting is vital to the success of your search engine optimization campaigns.

Negative Link Juice

When you acquire an inbound link, the authority it passes to your website is often referred to as "link juice". This term has been part of search engine optimization for as long as I can remember. It describes the value of a link passing value to your website in a positive manner. But what happens if you are acquiring links from less than desirable websites, blogs, or other digital assets? In the past, Google didn't really care if you received links from shady websites but this has changed over time. This means that if you're receiving a number of links from sites considered untrustworthy, then Google may be penalizing your rankings.

A common question that surfaces on a regular basis when it comes to the influence of inbound links is, "Does this mean that if I point a number of bad links at a website I can hurt their ranking?" Not really, Google has lessened their emphasis on the influence of SPAM sites linking to you. This happened a number of years ago when they took a leap in identifying unscrupulous websites and link farms. Google has been documented as saying they no longer pass negative link juice onto seemingly innocent websites but the jury is still out. At the time of this edition, Google still hasn't removed their tool for disavowing these links. Until they do, the best strategy is to monitor Google Console for manual actions against your site for unnatural links to your site. If that occurs, you can use the Disavow Links tool to alert Google.

What can you do to maintain a positive link profile?

There are a number of techniques you can use to eliminate any negative link juice and maintain a healthy link profile for your websites, blogs, and other digital asses. Doing so proactively will help protect against any inbound link issues or penalties in the future. The following are my recommendations for cleaning up your inbound links and optimizing your link building campaigns for long-term success.

1. Review your existing inbound link profile. The best way to get started is to see what your current link profile looks like. This means identifying all of the links currently pointing to your site and evaluating them from the perspective of website quality and anchor text. There are a large variety of tools on the market that do this including MOZ's Open Site Explorer, SEMrush, Cemper, etc. You can even use Google to give you a list of "links" but you're specifically looking for tools that provide inbound links and information about those links. In particular, what is the anchor text of each of the inbound links to your website?

2. Identify untrustworthy inbound links. Moz, SEMrush, and Cemper all provide a metric that allows you to determine the overall trust associated with each of the websites linking to you. The primary goal is to identify which links are untrustworthy in the eyes of Google and have them removed. At first glance, you may have some difficulty discerning which links are not fit for providing positive link juice. However, this is why it's so important to use a software tool as opposed to trying to figure it out on your own. Both of the before mentioned resources flag sites with little or no trust or authority.

3. Remove untrustworthy links. When I first went down this path of removing links it felt very awkward. I spent most of my SEO career building quality inbound links to my various websites, blogs, and other assets. Unfortunately, given the new Google updates, a number of these links were no longer supporting my goal of creating website authority so they had to go. The best way to remove a link is to do it yourself. If you've been submitting to article or directory sites that were negatively impacted by search engine algorithm updates, remove the link by logging into your profile and delete your post.

When you are unable to access links that have been deemed negative, you should browse the site to find a way to contact the website administrator. Submit a request that says, "Based on Google's latest update, I've been working to update my link profile and request to have my links removed from your website." Be sure to include the *specific link, anchor text*, and *webpage* where the link is found - don't expect someone else to do this for you. Be polite and gracious. More often than not your link is removed.

4. Use the Google Disavow Links Tool. Once you've gone through the process of manual link removal, visit Google Webmaster tools. There you will find a very helpful tool to disavow negative links to your website. Google quickly realized after their algorithm update that even if you follow steps 1 – 3 above, there may still be an issue with sites that are either unwilling to take down your link or intentionally trying to negatively impact your rankings. To that end Google introduced the *Disavow Links Tool*, available through Google Search Console. The tool lets you specify inbound links you want blocked and provides instructions on how to identify them.

Begin by visiting the Disavow links page within webmaster tools. When you arrive, you'll select your site from the dropdown list provided.

The next step is to upload a comprehensive file that includes the links you want to block or disavow.

The process of creating a file for upload is relatively simple. Personally, I was able to identify all of the links I needed blocked using link evaluation software and placed them in a spreadsheet that I saved as a text file. All that's required for disavow link submission is a text file with one URL per line.

For example:

```
# requested link removal but got no response
domain:baddomain1.com
# Webmaster of baddomain2.com removed most links,
but missed
http://www.baddomain2.com/contentA.html
http://www.baddomain2.com/contentB.html
http://www.baddomain2.com/contentC.html
```

In this example, lines that start with a pound sign "#" are considered comments and Google ignores them. The "domain:" keyword indicates that you want to disavow links from all pages on a particular website (in this case, "baddomain1.com"). You can also request to disavow links on individual webpages. In the example above, this is indicated by the three individual pages on baddomain2.com. Google currently allows only one disavow file per website. If you've already submitted a file and want it updated, you must first download, update, and then resubmit.

Google will encourage you to use the information in your Webmaster Tools account to begin researching links. Although Google Console is a great resource for finding all incoming links to your site, you'd have to visit each one and make a guess as to whether or not it's considered SPAMMY. In my opinion this takes way to long and is far too inaccurate. Use software to help you identify sites with zero trust or authority and include them in your file, Google takes care of the rest.

5. Build links from quality sites. Once you've done the work of removing unsavory links, it's time to start building quality inbound links to your website. A good portion of this book is dedicated to the practice of link building so I won't go into details here. The most important thing to remember is to build links based on quality, not quantity. Creating just a few links from quality sites can start to have a positive impact on your organic search results. Over time, development of quality inbound links that are do-follow in nature produce the best organic results. Do-follow means that links are crawled versus blocked by Google crawlers.

6. Create a natural inbound link profile by varying anchor text. Google's Penguin update was really about identifying unnatural link profiles. Through research and case studies it's relatively clear that branded anchor text is the primary goal. Descriptive anchor text has taken a back seat but is still important. Strive for anchor text that is around 70% branded (including your company name and/or URL) and 30% focused on descriptive keywords.

One final note in the area of addressing negative link juice. A number of SEO's have started to build links to 301 redirect pages. The benefit of building links to a page, other than your home page or any active page on your site is that a 301 redirect can be shut off at any time. Said another way, if you build links to an independent page on your server and redirect that page to your home or top level pages (301 redirect), you have total control over inbound links - the 301 can be shut off at any time. This is an advanced technique and one that truly isn't necessary but represents a creative way to manage third party links. Personally I prefer to use the Google Disavow links tool, allowing webmaster to "turn off" poor incoming links easily. Focus your efforts on building quality links, disavowing bad links when identified, and you'll be successful at managing your inbound link profile.

How to Get Links to Your Website

As I mentioned earlier, building links to your website is the most important aspect of improving your Google search results—bar none! It also provides a significant boost to improving your search engine result placements for multiple pages of your website.

When I started out in SEO, I never realized just how important inbound links were to Google or how to acquire quality links to my website in the right way. As a result I spent thousands of dollars, not to mention years of trial and error, to figure out that the more quality inbound links I developed, the higher my website would rank on Google.

When thinking about acquiring inbound links, and those links pointing to your website from other websites, there are two key principles to keep in mind.

Principle #1: Quality attracts quality. When it comes to search engine optimization, if you take the time to do things right the first time, you will achieve your goal. An example of this would be the process of asking a related website for a link that includes your keyword phrase(s). If you send a form letter or brief email and ask for a link exchange, there's a high probability you won't get it. However, if you take a few minutes to look at the website you're targeting and identify an opportunity to deliver something of sufficient value (exclusive content, social mention, interview, etc.) you have a much better chance of getting what you want. This is especially true if the site you are targeting is related to your niche or the products, services, or solutions you offer.

Acquiring quality links requires some effort. But don't despair, as I'll teach you in the next section, some link acquisition techniques are easier than others and can be outsourced. This helps you prioritize link building efforts and only focus on those initiatives that have a positive impact on your rankings. At the end of the day, a few high quality links will help you much more than tons of irrelevant links from low quality sites. Always focus on quality sites that can provide mutual benefit.

Principle #2: Persistence pays off. As I teach you the techniques I've used to improve my ranking on Google for even the most competitive phrases, think back to this principle again and again. Persistence is the key for achieving your desired result. Additionally, know that slow and steady wins the race. In fact, Google penalizes sites that seem to generate a bunch of links in just a very short period of time. This is why I avoid the, "too good to be true offer" where link builders promise hundreds or thousands of inbound links to your website. Even it they could provide such a result, you wouldn't want it. As soon as you start generating links, the Google algorithm is again looking for organic growth. This means adding links over time on a consistent basis.

A great example of this is some work I was doing for an online services company. After analyzing their website and suggesting some changes, I quickly realized that my on-page optimization recommendations would never be implemented—largely due to a bureaucratic web development team and their inability to handle multiple projects simultaneously. Over time I have found this situation to be more the norm than the exception.

Despite an inability to implement my on-page suggestions, I moved forward by coaching the marketing staff on the most basic on-page updates and then focusing on off-page optimization techniques for improving Google search engine results. We immediately started implementing these techniques on a regular basis to help their site increase rankings for specific search terms.

Truthfully, nothing happened for about eight weeks…and then WHAM! The techniques they used for building links to their website took hold and the results were undeniable. One of the keyword phrases that was most important to them went from the bottom of page 2 on Google to the number three position. Based on the results, it forced the internal team to make the requested on-page suggestions which improved results to an even greater degree.

Today, *everyone is looking for a quick fix*. And when it comes to SEO, there are a number of so-called quick fixes out there. These concepts are often referred to as *black hat* techniques and more often than not result in getting your website banned from all the major search engines. That's right. A lot of the attractive techniques for improving your rankings can have negative consequences. That's why it's so important to understand what you're doing and not chase the next SEO gimmick. Achieving top search engine placements is like losing weight. If you go on a starvation diet, sooner or later you're going to gain back all the weight you've lost and then some.

On the other hand, change you're eating and exercise habits slowly over time and you can create lasting health. The same principle applies here. Top rankings do not happen overnight. When you see a promise of "page one rankings in 24 hours", realize that it's a band aide, a temporary solution that might have a negative long-term impact on your website. Don't risk it. I've seen these empty promises come and go- they never end well. Instead, focus on developing links that are of good quality, quantity, and diversity. As time goes on and you achieve top rankings, it requires little additional effort to stay there. Be persistent and the results will stand the test of time as your site gains authority.

It's worth repeating here that Google has already identified situations where users are trying to game the system. This is especially true with link building. Remember that Google has data from billions of sites, all generating either inbound or outbound links. They not only know which links are valid, but the pace at which quality links are built for different types of sites within different niche markets. If you think you're going to fool Google, you're not. But we can play their game and win. This is why we start with on page optimization and site performance before focusing on link building and off-page optimization.

Pace yourself. When you're building a website or online business, you're in it for the long-haul and you don't want to put your website in jeopardy. Following these white-hat strategies are the best way to see results without incurring unnecessary risk.

Now that we've covered some basics about link-building, the foundation to off page optimization. Let's explore link development and other off page strategies in more detail. Look for a technique that resonates with you and learn all you can about that specific technique. Trying to learn it all at once or implement every technique is a fool's errand. Some will work for you and some will come more easily than others. I encourage you try them all but focus on those which come more easily as part of your search engine optimization efforts.

SEO Made Simple Off-Page Techniques

Let's jump right into it. All of these off-page optimization techniques will help improve your Google SERPs through link building, the most effective search engine optimization strategy available today. The more you use these proven techniques, the faster you'll see results. Don't hesitate—start using off-page optimization techniques immediately to build quality links to your website and watch your Google search engine results start to climb.

A word of caution. To be successful with off-page optimization, you MUST build your links slowly over time. Creating (or buying) dozens or hundreds of links can result in a Google penalty. I've seen it happen time and again. Despite sharing my experience with others in the hopes of helping them avoid the worst, I still receive emails that say, "I don't know what happened. All I did was buy 1,000 links from a guy on Fiverr and now my sight doesn't appear on Google." Be smart, be patient, have fun. Link building can be enjoyable and dramatically improve your organic results but you have to be focused on outcomes, not shortcuts.

What follows are the most effective techniques I've developed for acquiring quality links and improving rankings. In fact, applying each of these techniques properly can save you time while making the greatest impact on your rankings. Read through each of the techniques and give each one a try. You'll likely discover a few that you enjoy working with right off the bat. Start there and expand your efforts to include as many techniques as you can for lasting results.

Content Marketing

Content is king. And when it comes to search engine optimization, producing original content is your key to success. This is largely due to the significant changes we've seen in the Google algorithm over the past two years. As the algorithm has evolved, it's forced SEO's like myself to get really clear on our goals and produce a very targeted content strategy that will attract the type of individuals we want interacting with us and sharing our content.

Websites thrive on publishing new content that is targeted to their audience and niche. Using fresh, original content to develop inbound links to your website, blog, or other digital assets, is one of the most powerful optimization methods available. It's also a great place to start any search engine optimization initiative.

Although the area of "Content Marketing" is now very popular in SEO circles, it's actually been around for quite some time. Originally referred to as article marketing —the practice of writing articles within a given subject and distributing those to information-hungry websites across the web, has been a common practice for many years. Google has evolved their thinking on article marketing however, moving away from traditional article directories to focusing on original website content in various formats including: blog posts, images, video, PDFs, and other digital assets. The goal of content marketing is to share content on your site, and other websites, that is attributed to YOU. This attribution may come in the form of an *inbound link* to your website or use of an *author tag.* Either way, when others link to your website through content, your website gains valuable link juice that influences organic rankings.

With the addition of position zero, sometimes it's not even about sharing or distributing your content but making sure you're answering important questions that your audience is in search of. Using long form, organizing your content properly, and optimizing your on-page factors are essential for having a chance to appear at the top of SERPs. However, not every piece of content you create will be a fit for position zero. That's when you want to seek out other sites that might be interested in sharing your content with their audience or audience partners.

Content distribution sites use a basic concept that provides a number of SEO related benefits. Even though the authority of content distribution sites in general has been limited by Google over the last few years, they are still a good way for brand new websites to begin the link building process. When used properly, content distribution resources not only give you a link back to your website when content is published, they also distribute your information to third party websites and webmasters seeking content. This happens by registering with some kind of content aggregator, adding your content to the relevant category on their site, and submitting it for review. One of the more popular type(s) of content distribution sites currently in favor are blog networks. By joining a blog network (ex: BlogDash), you can write and distribute guest blog posts on a variety of websites.

Once your content has been submitted, reviewed, and approved for publishing, it's posted on a blog and sometimes distributed to website networks. The benefit of a guest post isn't the content itself but rather embedded links back to your website. **You leverage this content marketing method by including a link back to your website in the *About the Author* section using the proper link text (which includes your URL or keyword phrase[s]) or using the rel=**

"author" tag. The *author tag* links your content to your Google profile.

Each of these content distribution sites allows you to include an *About the Author* section at the conclusion of your article (see example on next page). You can see that I embedded links back to my website at the end of this sample article. Sometimes the author section has a header that says *About the Author* and other times it just appears at the end of the article. Don't submit an article without some type of link back to your website or tag that indicates the author. This is where the true value of content marketing comes into play for SEO. The main goal is to acquire a link back to your website – passing authority from a third party website to your own website or a specific web page.

The best part is that this link-building activity costs little or nothing to implement but carries a lot of impact. Keep in mind that you don't need to rely on blog networks to distribute your content. Research authoritative blogs in your niche and send an email to the blog owner with ideas for guest posts, results of a study you completed, an interview, or other exclusive content they can't find anywhere else.

Rel= "author" Tag

The second opportunity to leverage content marketing is to use the *author tag*. The concept is fairly simple and I'm sure you've already seen what it looks like when someone tags their content appropriately. Using the author tag not only helps your content stand out in search engine results but also gives you credit for that content wherever it appears on the Internet.

I strongly recommend using the tag on content published to your own website primarily as well as guest posts. This is to protect against others copying your content and claiming it as their own. It will also increase the popularity of your content specifically click-through rates, when appearing in search result listings. Tagging on third party sites using this method is less important but may be used selectively and is a great way to build an association between you and your content.

To claim content, be sure to link authored articles and posts to your Google My Business profile or other social sharing accounts. Go one step further and add a link to your blog, for example, in your email signature and anywhere it can generate exposure to your content. Don't expect someone else to find your content, proactively share it wherever you can.

When you do, you will increase visits and engagement with your content. Additionally, if the content is formatted correctly and includes social sharing icons, it will benefit from additional shares, signaling authority, helping it rank in search results.

Get noticed as a content provider

When you distribute your content and take the proper actions necessary to ensure its protection, you are following SEO best practices and giving your own website a boost in the SERPs. The added value of content distribution is that in addition to getting links to your website from the article site, you also get the viral effect provided when others post your content attributed back to you via inbound links and possibly an author tag.

The *viral effect* is when a webmaster sees you as a contributor and reaches out to you for content they can publish on their own website. Over time, web visitors may point to guest content on his site or copy and paste the article onto their own websites or blogs, generating even more one-way links back to your website.

To see the true effect of article marketing, search on Google for one of my many marketing articles from years ago, "7 Proven Strategies for Improving Your Alexa Ranking." You'll find more than eight thousand references to this article, many of which are from quality websites. The result, because many of these sites have my Author Box included at the bottom of the article, is thousands of one-way links pointing to one of my very first websites, with just a single article! It's like link building on steroids. Each link builds my website popularity and is essential for improving results on each of the major search engines.

Before you begin a content strategy, think about your area of expertise, relevant sites you'd like to approach with content ideas, and how to position yourself as an expert. After you've narrowed the search by utilizing a blog network or researching sites on your own, the next step is to reach out and start writing.

What if you don't have anything to write about?

Before developing content for your website or blog, there are a few things you can do to get started. Truthfully the best place to start is with trending topics like those you can find on *Google Trends, Reddit,*

Buzz Sumo, and virtually any social network. I've spent a lot of time working with companies who are struggling with content generation and learned a few things about developing and distributing content effectively for SEO purposes. In particular, I have found the following to have an immediate and lasting impact on any content management program.

1. **Editorial Calendar.** An editorial calendar is essential for any website owner. Your goal, the goal of your website, should be to develop *topical authority*. Topical authority means that in your niche, you're producing and distributing targeted content that matters to your audience. This content can be distributed as an article, blog post, image, infographic, video, audio recording, etc. Regardless of the format you chose, your goal is to produce something that's relevant and often planned. Creating spontaneous content is good because it allows you to leverage the news or emerging trends, but evergreen content is effective for long-term SEO. This is why an editorial calendar is so important to the optimization of your website.

   Developing an editorial calendar is simple. Start with a blank sheet of paper, spreadsheet, post-it, or napkin. Write down 12 different topics related to your niche. For example, if you are focused on health and wellness, you may write down things like: the healthiest foods, dieting, exercise, sleep habits, maintaining the health of your vehicle, etc. You know your area of expertise better than anyone else so choose popular, evergreen topics, you write or comment about.

   The next step is to come up with 2-3 ideas per month that you can talk about and decide how you will deliver your content. Whether you write a blog post or record a video with your mobile device, the goal is to stay focused around a particular topic or keyword and consistently produce content for distribution. The more focused your content, the quicker you'll develop a deep reservoir of expertise and authority on the topic.

   As you work through your editorial calendar week after week and month over month, focus on distribution. Use your website and social media channels to distribute your content to a targeted audience. As you package and distribute your content, you'll be creating a larger footprint on the internet and providing more opportunities for individuals and other websites to point back to your site.

2. Amplify.

The second thing to consider is amplification. Once you make the effort to develop content, you must create a strong interest in and awareness of your content. The only way to do this is to increase your reach. There are two primary organic ways to achieve amplification. The first is using social media and the second is through the use of influencers.

Each time you create new content on your website or for a third party site, leverage existing social media channels to amplify the content – push it out to those who are interested in consuming it. This could take the form of share buttons near the content you are trying to amplify (ex: AddThis.com) or posting on your Google, Facebook, Linkedin, and Twitter accounts and pages. As you post the information, others will share it with their networks.

The second way to amplify content is to leverage influencers in your market. Find people with influence and ask them to contribute by writing a guest post for your website or being interviewed for publication or podcast, allowing you to share their expertise. After completing the work with this individual, ask them to distribute the content you've created with their audience. You'd be amazed at the impact of having an existing authority endorse and promote your content.

Help with content

If you are struggling to write your own content, there are some tools to help you find things to write about that stem from your chosen keywords. Sites like *Answer the Public* or *Google Trends* can be quite helpful in getting ideas flowing.

If you're not a writer or don't have the time to put into content creation, you can also hire an agency, freelancer, or ghostwriter to develop content on your behalf. In fact, a much larger portion of our workload at Big Fin SEO, is focused on producing content for clients. From blog posts to custom images and video, content generation has become an essential part of search engine optimization. This is due to the changes to the Google algorithm we've discussed, giving more value to sites producing valuable, engaging content on a regular basis.

Even if you're a small business, I recommend budgeting time or dollars to generate content on an ongoing basis. Unfortunately it's become table stakes in the game of SEO. Updating your site once year is no longer an option. Rather, producing content on a daily or weekly basis helps your site continually expand, provides more value to website visitors, and helps you to stay current. If you don't have time, or the talent to update your site with new content on a regular basis, I strongly recommend finding a dependable resource. Whether it's you, a member of your staff, or an agency, it's important to your SEO success.

If you're looking for someone to simply write for you, instead of manage your overall SEO, I would recommend using a popular site called *Upwork.com*. You could likely negotiate with someone depending on your topic and pay as little as $25 per blog post, image, or info graphic.

Writing original content or having original content developed for you can be worth *every* cent. For me, article creation, blog posts, and presentations have created thousands of links back to my websites. In fact, if you Google my name *Michael Fleischner,* in addition to authoritative websites being listed you'll find tens of thousands of references associated with my blog posts and content marketing which has traditionally been one of my favorite SEO strategies.

I have evolved my content marketing techniques over the past few years to save time while improving effectiveness. Additionally, changes in how content is viewed by search engines like Google has modified the way I use this strategy by focusing only on the top websites in my niche, creating 100% unique content, and distributing content on a regular basis.

It is widely reported that Google penalizes sites for publishing duplicate content. To avoid these penalties, it's important that you create unique content that can be shared and posted online. A good habit to get into is to use the rel=author tag if writing for another website or blog. This gives you claim to the content as your own. Once you begin distributing the content, make sure that each submission is unique. Doing so increases the chances that your content gets published online and provides the "link juice" you want from your content marketing efforts.

The challenge with unique content is that even if you have an original article and publish to your own website, that content is no longer unique. What happens when you start submitting to third-party sites? How can you create unique content each time you submit or share an article? The answer to that question is a concept called *Article Spinning.*

Spinning an article means that you use a tool to generate multiple unique articles from a single article. Although not as popular as it once was, article spinning is an option if you have a limited budget and are willing to put in the time to edit your article revisions.

The way article spinning works is simple. You begin by writing or having someone write for you an original article or piece of content. From that one article you create multiple, unique versions before submitting to article directories. There are a variety of spinners on the market that help you with this process. I recommend using a spinner (that can create an article that is 70% unique or better) if you are manually submitting to other blogs or content distribution sites.

There are a variety of services that can help you write, spin, and distribute content. Although Google has devalued many traditional article resources, having the ability to generate original content is still incredibly valuable, especially among blog networks. Additionally, content creation goes way beyond articles. Think of all the different types of content you interact with online from video to social media. When it comes to content, regardless of the type, pace yourself. This ensures that links aren't built too quickly, resulting in the Google penalty.

The key to link building is to establish inbound links to your site in a slow and steady manner. This is especially true with content marketing. Keep in mind that tools which help with content distribution generally submit a large batch of articles or blog posts all at once. This is a bad idea – throwing up links on low authority websites quickly is a sure way for Google to stand up and take notice that you're intentionally trying to game the system. Remember that Google is watching. Content distribution is valuable for building inbound links and website authority if done over an extended period of time. Your pace is up to you as long as it's done gradually.

In my opinion, content marketing is a great way for any website to start building links and get your site noticed. Remember however, you must use original content and limit your submissions to only the top directories, blogs, or forums. You want only quality links, so take your content creation seriously. I suggest creating one to two blog posts per week and distributing them to top sites in your niche for publication. This can increase your SERPs both short and long-term if done properly and consistently over time.

As you get more comfortable with content creation, start to look for new or innovative ways to distribute your content. You'd be surprised by how many websites or bloggers would like to have new, original content on a regular basis. Research sites in your niche and contact them offering free, original content in exchange for a link back to your website. These partnerships can have a significant impact on your website authority, ranking, and even your owner personal brand. Some of the partnerships I've developed for content distribution have also turned into join venture partnerships and good friends. Continue to network and seek out opportunities in your niche.

Asking for Links

Unfortunately link exchanges are a bit outdated but certainly not dead. One of the fastest ways to build links to your website, and therefore link popularity, is through *reciprocal link building* when applied correctly. As we discussed in an earlier section, there are essentially three types of links: one-way, reciprocal, and three-way. One-way links are the links you acquire that point directly to your site. We are discussing a number of methods for acquiring one-way links, such as content marketing because they are often the most powerful type of link you can acquire. Reciprocal links are created when two websites agree to link to each other. Reciprocal links are also known as *link swaps, link exchanges*, and *link partners*. When I was first starting out in search engine optimization I used reciprocal linking to establish a number of quality links to my website.

The challenge here is that a reciprocal link is really only valuable if the MozRank or MozTrust of the site that's linking to you is greater or equal to the rating of your own website. That's not to say that links from established sites with low ratings don't provide value. In fact, when you're starting out, every inbound link from an established website helps!

In the last couple of years, the concept of basic reciprocal linking has fallen out of favor. However, I believe that you need to use a combination of link-building strategies if you ever wish to achieve top search engine placements for your desired keyword phrases. Entertaining the concept of link exchanges and requests still has merit, especially for newer websites.

When you're developing reciprocal links, seek out websites that are contextually relevant to yours. In other words, if your site is about clothing, seek out other sites dedicated to apparel. These sites will tend to have similar content (keywords) to your site embedded in title tags, body copy, on-page links, and so on. This is a real positive in the eyes of Google and other major search engines.

Google favors links from sites that share the same or similar theme as your website, increasing the value of each incoming link. The more time you spend seeking out relevant link partners, the better.

Reciprocal Links and How to Get Them

Before asking any site for a link exchange, you'll need to develop a linking strategy. A good place to start is to develop a resources page or recommendation page on your own website. This page, also referred to as a partner or resource page is where you'll be placing the links to those sites that place one or more of your links on their website. As a rule of thumb, never include more than twenty links on your resources page as Google may consider your page to be a link farm. Link farms are in the business of posting links to other sites for a fee. Google has pretty much eliminated all link farms at this point so those which remain are simply wolves in sheep's clothing. Being association with this type of site is a negative ranking factor and one you must avoid. Most importantly, **place a link to your resources page from your home or other top-level page**.

Linking from your home page will transfer the authority of your home page, which usually has the highest authority rating of any page on your website, to your resources page—making it all that more valuable to potential link partners. This is also a great strategy if you're promoting affiliate products and want to pass a lot of authority to that page as well. Linking directly from the home page to important pages, as part of the navigation or through some other means, is a great way to elevate the authority and ranking of the page.

After you've created a page to place links, it's time to find some link exchange partners or sites who might be interested in linking to what you offer – usually in the form of free content. Begin by identifying a site that would be an appropriate link partner. E-mail the webmaster of the site by locating a *Contact Us* button, form, or the webmaster's e-mail address.

Before you send an e-mail requesting a link or link exchange, place a link to the targeted website on your resources page. Doing so shows the webmaster of the site that you're serious about a link exchange and willing to take the first step. If the webmaster says no, you can always remove their link from your links page. Here is a sample e-mail you can use when contacting webmasters:

Dear Webmaster,

My name is _____ and I am the webmaster of [PUT YOUR WEBSITE URL HERE]. I have visited your site [URL HERE] and believe it would be a valuable resource for my website browsers.

I'd like to exchange links with you and have already added a link to your website on my links page at [INSERT URL WHERE YOU PLACED LINK]. I would ask that you provide a link back to my website in return. Doing so would offer a valuable resource to your website's visitors and improve website authority for both of us.

If you are interested in exchanging links or recommending each other as resources, please add the following details to your website and let me know when you have done so. The details of our site are given below:

Title: Your keyword phrase here
URL: http://yourwebsiteurl.com

Description: [Place a description of your website here. Make sure you include your primary keyword phrase at least two times in a manner that seems natural].

Alternatively, you can just copy the html code

<a href=http://www.yourwebsite.com rel="dofollow" target="_blank">Your keyword phrase</a> *Place a description of your website here. Make sure you include your primary keyword phrase at least two times in a manner that seems natural.*

If you are not interested in completing a link exchange at this time, please let us know and we will remove your link from our links page which has proven a valuable resource for our current partners. Thank you for your consideration.

Kind Regards
[your first name]

Feel free to modify this e-mail as you like and be sure to vary anchor text. The key with contacting any webmaster is to sound genuine and act in good faith. As I mentioned in Principle #1, quality attracts quality and in #2, persistence pays off. You'll receive more 'no' answers than 'yes' answers, but over time yeses add up and you'll have plenty of quality links pointing to your website!

Based on the type of website you have, the value of the resources provided, or how well established your site is, you may consider sending a link request without the promise of a reciprocal link. A one-way link is much more valuable than a reciprocal link, but websites aren't always willing to provide you with a free link unless they see you as a well-established authority website.

On a final note, once you establish a link exchange, check back regularly to make sure the reciprocal link is in place. If your link has been removed, contact the webmaster to inquire as to why your link was removed. Keep in mind that you want the value of the inbound links to your links page to be greater than the value of the outbound links; always make sure a reciprocal link is in place. If not, remove the site from your links page in order to maintain positive link value.

Three-Way Link Exchange

The next type of link exchange is called a three-way link exchange and should be your goal when engaging in link development. As noted in the previous section, "Link Types," a three-way link exchange is similar to creating a one-way link to your site. This can be handled in a similar manner to our reciprocal link exchange— sending an email to the webmaster defining your intentions. I can tell you definitively that if you spend the time to find a relevant site and have a secondary asset (another website or blog) you can use to generate a one-way link to your prospective link partner, then three-way links should be a preferred strategy for you.

Three-way link exchanges work in the following manner. You link to someone else's website from a secondary asset you own. This could be another website or blog. Once the link is in place, you request that a link point back to your primary website. Using this strategy, you are receiving a one-way link from the third party site to your primary website, not the one that contains the outbound link. By developing one-way links through a three-way link exchange, you are optimizing the value of your link building campaign by passing inbound link value to your primary website.

The key to being successful with link exchanges is always to think about value and relevance. Try to acquire links from third-party sites in your niche that have authority, age, or number of inbound links.

Relying on three-way link exchanges is a great way to steadily improve website authority. In fact, it's a relatively quick way to generate quality links pointing to your main website.

Keep in mind that you don't always have to exchange text links either. You can embed links in images, assets, slides, etc. It's more important that you understand the concept and look for link exchange opportunities than it is the type of link you create. Any URL pointing to your site is going to help in some way if it's of decent quantity so be open minded and experiment.

BONUS: In bound links are still vitally important to the success of your SEO campaign. Many of the websites we optimize benefit from targeted link campaigns. For example, one client developed a savings calculator that was unique to people in their 50s – focusing on catch up contributions and other financial instruments designed to accelerate their savings. A different client built an inexpensive tool that would help would-be buyers make the right choice of security systems for their home. Spend some time thinking about useful tools for your audience and then share that tool with others in your industry who will link directly to the tool on your website. This goes a long way in developing inbound links without the heavy lifting of asking potential link partners to do you a favor.

Once you've mastered the skill of link exchanges, it's time to focus your energy on building meaningful links with an arsenal of optimization strategies. In the next section we'll focus on effective strategies for building links over the long term. This is the goal when it comes to Google because much of the algorithm is based on trends with your website. Think recency, frequency, and longevity. As I always advise clients, slow and steady wins the race. You might think its self-serving as most SEO companies make their money one monthly services but it happens to be the way Google works when it comes to identifying and favoring authoritative websites.

Local Directories – Essential for Local Businesses

If you're going to own and operate a website, you must take the time to submit your website to well-established, authoritative local search engines. There are tons of local search engines and directories that are having a significant impact on Google search results. This has evolved with the ever-changing landscape of mobile devices being used to surf the web. Local search is a great way to generate dozens of quality one-way links to your website regardless of target audience.

Traditional directories include sites which simply list business or website information. More recently, these traditional directories have evolved to support the explosion of mobile search and those looking for products and services within a given geography. For example, the most popular of these newer directories is *Google My Business*. This business directory supports local search and turns up in search results for most location based queries.

First, let me give you the history on traditional website directories. When thinking about traditional directories, there are generally two types: *human-edited* and *automated*. Human-edited directories review each website submission by hand and upon acceptance list websites by category. These directories were once considered high quality and integral in the Google authority rating. The most popular of all human-edited directories is DMOZ (which no one uses anymore) but it set the tone for the use of directories and listing sites.

Another type of traditional directory is the automated directory. Automated directories are basically a dime a dozen and at this point, having your website listed on them could result in a penalty from search engines. Although traditional directories like these have created some SEO value in the past, I would avoid them. Remember, even if a directory submission is free, you want to focus on submitting to *quality* directories—sites with an established authority, age, appropriate categories, and so on. In general, automated directories are nothing but link farms and don't carry much weight today.

Consider that many human and automated directories work on a concept of link exchange. To get listed in their directory, you must provide a link to the directory from your website's link page. As the value of traditional link exchanges have diminished, so has the value of these old school directories.

The new improved directory options.

The traditional directory has evolved into the local business directory – and they are thriving. These new and improved local directories have been optimized for mobile and local search and carry a great deal of website authority of their own.

Local search directories are focused on driving targeted search results to businesses that are within a certain geographic radius of where you're searching from. Local search has exploded in recent years because of Google's integration of local business information into search results on mobile and desktop devices. This is a trend that will continue to grow and expand for years to come.

The number of local search directories has exploded and should be integrated into every company's search engine optimization program. Today, this is the number one recommendation I make to clients who want to improve their online presence, boost organic search results on Google, and develop quality inbound links to their websites- get listed on local search directories!

Enter Data Aggregators

There are a number of companies that have been leading the local search transition from static directories. The most popular, created by Google is called *Google My Business*. Other robust services have emerged as well, making submission to popular local search engines both simple and highly effective.

These directories and services have come under the term, "Data Aggregators". Simply put, a data aggregator collects information from a business and distributes it to a select group of high profile, very authoritative, local search engines and/or directories. The most popular, Google My Business, is used to collect information from businesses and display that information in search results for relevant queries. Services like Bright Local and Moz Local go one step further and submit your business information to the top local search engines. Google uses information from these local search directories to validate and sometimes display their own results.

Google My Business

If you only do one things for your business from an SEO perspective, do this! Go to www.google.com/mybusiness and register for a FREE directory listing. That's right, a directory listing. As I mentioned previously, directories aren't dead, they've simply evolved and Google is leading the charge. The Google My Places directory is what commands the majority of search engine results for local searches. In fact, you can begin generating more traffic to your website in as little as 48 hours after confirming your account simply by registering your business with *Google My Business* and optimizing your profile. This is so important that I'm going to explain the process and make it really simple for you.

1. Do you have a gmail account? If not, go to gmail.com and register for one. It's free.
2. Go to www.google.com/business
3. Register by searching for your business and either selecting a location or indicating that you are a new business. If you do not have a storefront, list your home address.
4. Enter basic information about your business (address, phone, etc.)
5. Submit. Once you enter your information, Google will send a post card to your house or business address within a few weeks to verify your existence. The post card includes a confirmation number that needs to be entered online. When you receive the card, follow instructions for verification.

That's it! Once verified, your listing will appear in local search results in less than 48 hours. To optimize your listing, spend some time ensuring that all information is completed. Google definitely is preferred placement to more robust profiles including hours of operation, contact information, photos, etc.

In our work at Big Fin SEO, we've seen a huge improvement in search results when completing the Google My Business profile fully. This means taking the time to go through each area of the info tab and completing the information. From hours of operation to business category to services offered, make sure you leave no stone unturned.

This is your opportunity to position your business for success and control what others see in relation to your business. I'd place particular emphasis on photos. Recent studies have shown that Google My Business profiles with the most images get the majority of views, traffic, and engagement. We recommend encouraging customers to upload photos as well as posting your own on a regular basis. This could mean once a week, once a month, or every other month depending on your customer base, changes to your business, and other subjective factors.

The last part of your Google My Business profile, is asking for and responding to reviews. Don't be afraid to ask customers for reviews. They're going to leave them anyway. However, if you're proactive about asking for reviews, you can focus on clients who you know have had a positive experience. Building up a huge cache of positive reviews will offset any negative reviews that you will receive. And trust me, at some point you'll get one or more – it's just the nature of having a business. Keep in mind that no one is perfect and having a few negative reviews isn't the end of the world. What's most important is how you respond. For the clients we manage, we always respond to both positive and negative reviews. This helps with Google as it shows that you are actively managing your business.

Don't stop there

Google My Business is just one of many local search directories, albeit the largest and most influential. However, Google also relies on second tier directories to verify and supplement search engine results. Submitting your site to other local directories has a number of benefits from and SEO perspective. When your site is included on other directories you enjoy many benefits that boost search results:

- Your Business information more available on the web
- Your website appears in a variety of local search results
- Your site inherits authority from quality inbound links
- Your site receives validation for Google search algorithm

Getting listed in local search results is essential for website authority, improved presence online, and generating targeted website traffic. I've spent hundreds of hours presenting, discussing, and writing about the value of local search results for businesses with local, regional, and national reach. The reality is that local search directories have become too large to ignore with regard to their impact on organic search results.

Leveraging local search directories

There are a variety of local directories to choose from covering standard business directories, GPS sites, mobile directories, and mobile maps. So which do you choose? The two biggest questions I get are as follows: 1) What local search directories should I list my information on and, 2) How do I optimize my listing to ensure top ranking?

These questions are really the most important to consider because there are literally hundreds of local search directories and they are not all created equally. As mentioned previously, Google My Business carries the most weight, but other directories from Bing to Yelp to Yellow Pages pack a heavy punch. From my perspective, in addition to those mentioned, there are about 40 primary local search engines that carry significant weight and authority. Visit my secret resource page (URL in footer of each page) to access some of the most recent high authority local search directories available. **You can also visit a site like Moz Local which provides data aggregation services.**

The benefit of using a data aggregator is the ease by which you can submit your website's data and information to the leading local search directories. Many of these aggregators have direct feeds with the most influential directories, allowing for instant and ongoing updates to be made to your listing. The days of manually submitting your information to online directories is long gone – although some still choose to do it (I'm not sure why). For my clients, I've relied on data aggregators to do the heavy lifting and ensure my client's websites are both included and optimized on the MOST important local search directories influencing organic search results.

When submitting to local search directories, always make sure that your information appears in exactly the same way. Remember that Google is a machine that reads websites. If your phone number is different on each list or your abbreviate your address in some and not in other, for example "blvd." versus "boulevard", then Google will not see it as being the same and therefore may not pass the optimal link authority between your listing and website. One way to make sure that information appears exactly the same across high authority local search engines is by using a data aggregator. This ensures both placement and accuracy, two things which are vitally important with local search directories.

The reason why name, address, and phone number (NAP) consistency is so important is validation. Think of it this way. If you were a legitimate business, would you change your address or phone number frequently? Probably not. Google relies on consistent information being published about a business to validate legitimacy and eliminate spam.

When you take the time to get your site listed on local directories, whether you're a local business or not, you benefit in a variety of ways. Not only to some directory sites generate traffic directly from users, but they also distribute business information to other websites, increasing exposure for your business. The second, and probably the most important benefit is that you're acquiring high quality links to your website. Said another way, instead of going through the difficult process of seeking out link partners and acquiring one way links, you're able to buy them.

A final word on local search directories to keep you grounded. When submitting to local directories it is important to focus on quality over quantity. Keep your attention on authoritative directories and quality of information. When focused on traditional directories, be very selective. Only select data aggregators focused on the top directories not hundreds or thousands of directories that have little or no authority. Where people generally get into trouble is when they identify a large list of directories and submit to all of based on quantity, not quality. Often these lists are dated, do not include local search directories, and are "too good to be true". Place more of your link development on local search directories that are well established. Right now, Google is weighing businesses and websites more heavily if available on local search engines.

Reviews

If you are a local business or a company selling products or services of any kind, generating positive reviews for your business is absolutely critical. This is a growing factor in local search and no business, regardless of how well optimized their website may be, can take full advantage of Google without it.

I'm always amazed when people challenge me on the value of reviews. It's never a good idea to conduct, "market research of one" – meaning trusting your own opinion and no-one elses, but think about your own search behavior. Are you going to visit a doctor with 32 positive reviews or the doctor who has none? Worse yet, what if you see someone or something with dozens of negative reviews?

Even more important than the direct impact that reviews have on your business is the impact they have on your Google listings. Sites with more reviews tend to do better in local search results. This is especially true of your Google My Business listing but is also true in studies that look at local rankings and the correlation among sites with positive reviews and high levels of engagement on social media. If you haven't taken reviews seriously, now is the time to buckle down and take business reviews seriously.

There are a number of tools available for helping you ask for and receive reviews. These services essentially work in the following way:

1. You send an email or text message to a customer asking them to rate your service.

2. Those who provide a high rating (ex: 9 out of 10) are redirected to leave a review on a popular review site – Google My Business, Facebook, or Yelp.

3. The individual leaves a rating and review and you're notified.

The process is very simple but you need to implement it. At Big Fin SEO, we started implementing a great process with our clients a number of years ago, printing up business cards that companies could hand out to customers directing them to specific review sites. Whether you're looking to build reviews on Google or some other site, giving customers a physical reminder is a great step. Additionally, you can send a "5-star" link to customers asking them for a review. When our clients request reviews, we make sure they are sending a special URL that opens up their review page with 5 stars already filled in. This makes it easy for clients to leave a review and save.

I recommend always responding to reviews, positive and negative. It shows Google that you care about your customers and is generally a good practices. Be sure to take a proactive approach to review gathering, feedback, and management. Integrate reviews into your business processes. Don't leave this to chance especially if you're a local business. Building positive reviews is necessary for local search domination.

Blogging

Blogging provides SEO value from three distinct vantage points. By now you should know about blogging and maybe even have a blog of your own (to learn more about making money through blogging, check out *Blogging Made Simple* on Amazon.com). From a search engine optimization perspective, having your own blog provides a significant boost to your SEO efforts over time through additional website listings, content development, and social media. In this section, I'll also show you how to leverage your own blog and other people's blogs to build inbound links and increase your search engine rankings.

Let's begin our review of how to use blogs for SEO purposes by talking about setting up your own blog. Although creating your own blog isn't necessary, it does have a number of benefits that can't be overlooked. Once you create your own blog and that blog earns authority, you can start adding links and passing authority to any site you choose. For example, a number of years ago, I started "The Marketing Blog." Anytime I launch a new website or want to give a client some extra link juice, I simply make a post that includes a link to the third-party website. Essentially, by creating your own blog you are developing an authoritative resource you can use to pass authority and value to any site you are optimizing. This is a great long-term strategy that comes in handy when you want to quickly increase the rankings of new websites you are trying to get to the top of search result listings. Furthermore, Google loves links that are integrated into content (not just on the sidebar, a.k.a. blogroll). By placing links in the flow of text, you add value and importance to the link.

A number of years ago, after hearing about the popularity of blogs and learning about the multiple benefits of creating one, I set out to start my own blog. By doing some research, I found a number of popular websites that actually let you create and host your blog for free. What's even better is that the process of creating your blog is incredibly fast and easy. I suppose that's why blogging has become so popular. The following process is the best way to start and leverage your blog for maximum search engine optimization value.

Step 1: Choose a Purpose or Topic

One of the most important things you can do to ensure a quality blog is to determine the purpose and topics you will be posting about. For example, a number of individuals who host blogs simply want to share their ideas on a particular topic. Others are looking for an outlet to make posts on just about anything without a specific agenda. Often these latter individuals are seeking to create an online journal or revenue with Google AdSense (pay-per-click advertising), display advertising, or promotion of affiliate products.

Regardless of the purpose you choose, select a topic that allows you to contribute on a regular basis. For SEO purposes, choose a topic related to your niche. You'll have plenty of content ideas to write about or develop ideas based on comments readers submit. This is one of the best ways to develop new content relevant to readers and keeps them engaged, increasing web traffic and time on site.

Step 2: Select a Blog Provider

There are a number of websites that offer free blogs. Most websites however have the ability to blog or create posts within the site – so having a separate "blog" really isn't necessary any longer. Using your website to publish blog posts has become the norm. WordPress is now the standard in blogging platforms and includes endless plugins to add any type of functionality you want. You can host a WordPress blog on your own site (WordPress.org) or use their hosted service (WordPress.com). If you're not sure which to use I suggest you read *Blogging Made Simple* or visit YouTube to start watching videos related to blog setup. There you can get some insight into the different blogging platforms that are available and which works best for your blog topic.

Step 3: Launch Your Blog

If you're selecting a blog host like Blogger.com to launch your blog, all you do is create an account, name your blog, and choose a template. From there you can begin posting to your blog immediately. Many providers like Blogger.com give you the ability to choose from a number of basic templates. Advanced users can design their own blog templates to customize look and feel.

WordPress.com, now the preferred platform is also very simple to use. After creating a username and entering your e-mail address, you create a blog name and title. You'll receive a confirmation e-mail that provides instructions on how to begin.

Once you've launched your blog and made a number of posts, you should really focus on generating traffic. Not only will traffic support any online business you may have, but it can also improve the overall quality of your blog. Some simple techniques for generating traffic to your blog include:

- Design your blog for SEO using on-page optimization techniques. If using WordPress, install the All-in-One SEO pack or a similar plugin, allowing you to customize title tags, descriptions, and more

- Generate links to your blog via link exchange, content marketing, and traffic exchanges

- Update content on a daily or weekly basis.

- Use ping services like Ping-o-Matic to recognize new posts.

One thing you'll find about starting your own blog is that blogging is both simple and fun. As you develop a loyal readership, you'll find blogging to be a great learning experience as well. Simply put, there's no reason why you shouldn't start blogging today. This is especially true if you're trying to build your reputation or provide something of value in relation to your business. As you develop deep content and expertise, authoritative pages on your blog can be used to pass value to other website pages.

Once your blog is up and running, place a link from your blog's homepage to the website you are trying to optimize, including the keywords you are optimizing for. This will obviously help your Google ranking via the inbound link-building strategies we've been discussing, but you should wait until your blog has an established Google value before linking out to other websites. This can take a number of months so be patient. What you don't want to do is place an outbound link to your site day one without an established Google PR. Google may view the inbound link as spammy and penalize your site. Blog development is a long-term strategy but one that can serve you well in the search engine optimization game.

Blog Commenting

The second way to use blogs effectively for search engine optimization is through the concept of blog commenting. When you visit a blog related to your niche, most posts give you the option of leaving a comment. This may be available by clicking on a hyperlink that says "comments" or simply beneath a post itself. Blog commenting is a great way to acquire a one-way link to your website if done properly.

The first step is to find high authority blogs in your niche. It's important that the blogs you leave comments on are what we call "do follow" blogs. This means that the blog owner permits third-party links to be indexed by search engines, passing value from its pages to your website. Search Google for "High Authority Do Follow Blogs" or research blogs in your niche.

Once you have created a list of high authority, do follow blogs, you can begin leaving comments on appropriate posts. Here are a few tips for making the most of this strategy:

1. Enter your brand name or keyword in the field marked, "Name." This is the MOST important step in productive blog commenting.

2. Use a real email address for submission purposes.

3. Use a complete URL when listing your site address in the space provided. Do NOT include a URL in the actual comment.

4. Leave a comment that is directly related to the post, has substance, and is longer than three sentences.

5. Track all of your blog submissions and build a list of high PR, do follow blogs that you can return to from time to time. Always leave comments on different posts—never the same post.

As someone who manages a blog and uses blog commenting on a regular basis to build one-way links to my sites, I know how important the above guidelines are for making the most of blog commenting. When moderating comments for my own blog, I personally don't mind people using their keyword as the name (although some blogs won't allow this) and linking to their website in the URL field. In fact, I see it as a quid pro quo if they take the time to read my post and leave a valuable comment. However, I will delete their comment if they place a link in the body of the comment because it's usually SPAM.

Start searching for those blogs that can support your link building and be part of the conversation. You can add this strategy to the mix and start to see why link building can be fun and somewhat addictive.

Guest Posts

The third way to use blogging as a powerful optimization tool is through the process of submitting guest posts. This is one of my favorite and most powerful strategies for attracting third party links. If you are in-tune with niche-specific blogs and follow them on a somewhat regular basis, you should try for a guest post on the blog itself.

I've been successful in offering guest posts to third party blogs in exchange for links for nearly a decade. If you take a customized approach and are selective, you can really do well using this technique. This approach is effectives because blog owners are always looking for relevant, 100% unique content. Although guest post submissions take a little time and effort, it's well worth it. Some of my most powerful incoming links are from guest-related blog posts.

If there is a blog you'd like to target, write a 500 plus post on a relevant topic. Then, contact the blog owner and submit the post with your author profile using something like the following replacing bracketed text with your own:

Dear [blog name],

My name is [name] and I've been reading your blog for quite some time. I'm also heavily involved in [name of your niche] and have created a 100% original blogpost to share with your readers. I've read your guidelines and believe this post meets your submission standards.

I've attached the post for review. If you'd like to use it please let me know as I personally believe it would be a valuable topic to cover on [blog name]. If for some reason you do not want to share this information with your readers, I'd appreciate a response so I can offer the content to another blog.

I've also included a bio section with my picture and credentials. If you decide to use the post I ask that you include a link back to my site. If there are any concerns or issues, don't hesitate to contact me at [support@bigfinseo.com] or via phone at [(999) 555-1212].

Kind regards,

[name here]

P.S. I'm also on Skype under the name [skypename] if you would like to discuss this further.

By customizing your message and content, you're sure to get the attention of the blog owner. Additionally, by providing personal contact information, the blog owner knows you are legitimate. Target high authority blogs in your niche as well as newer blogs who may be seeking more content. Over time, your submissions will grow and you'll be valuable inbound links to your website.

Profile Sites – Authority Links

There are a variety of high authority sites available that allow you to post a link quickly and easily. In fact, I personally learned about high authority profile sites by accident. If it weren't for my need to experiment, I'd likely have overlooked this effective SEO technique and never had the opportunity to share it with you.

For a time I focused a lot of my energy on affiliate marketing. Even today I make a nice residual income with niche websites where I earn a commission each time a product or service is sold. A couple of years back I started searching for new ways to sell my own products and generate traffic to my niche websites. In short order, I stumbled upon a forum that included "special offers" from other Internet marketers. I liked the idea so much that I even added this feature to my SEO Community! One of the special offers had to do with access to a list of high authority websites where you could easily leave a link back to your website.

I purchased the list and found a bit of a mixed bag. Some of the sites were no longer active or only allowed you to leave a link on a dynamic page—which has little value—but most of the sites noted were legitimate and carried a great deal of authority. Ever since I first discovered this technique of finding and dropping links on high authority sites, which I call *Profile Sites*, I've relied on monthly submissions to help my rankings.

The reason I call these sites Profile Sites is because they are often based on forums, social Media sites, wikis, and other online resources that allow you to include a link with your registration profile. Upon completing your registration, you can include a link that is immediately accessible or available when you leave some type of comment or post on the site itself.

There are essentially 3 types of high profile sites. The first includes popular social media site (ex: Facebook, LinkedIn, Google+, etc.), the second includes broad authority sites (ex: Wikipedia.com, About.me, etc.), and the third, Industry-Specific sites (ex: ZocDoc).

We will be covering social media in a separate section so I won't spend too much time on it here but if you don't have a presence on Facebook, Twitter, and Google+, you're missing a huge opportunity to develop very powerful links to your website. On each of the before mentioned social channels, your profile allows links to websites of your choice. Make sure your profiles are up-to-date, complete, and link to your website's home page.

Broad authority sites are ideal for listing your website. These sites, like Wikipedia, may require some level of expertise to get listed, but it's usually worth it. If you search for "Michael Fleischner", you'll notice my Wikipedia page. I paid a Wikipedia expert to create my profile and get it listed. This is something I was unable to do myself. Sometimes it pays to make a small investment that pays huge dividends! There are other sites like Wikipedia that you should take advantage of for yourself and your business.

Personally I like Klout.com, About.me, and Crunchbase to name a few. Keep your eyes open for other authority sites you see coming up in your competitor's search results.

The third type of authority site is industry specific. The best example I can give are sites that have online listings for different types of professionals. If you're a doctor, dentist, or lawyer, there are countless websites that allow you to obtain an authoritative listing and inbound link to your very own website. Some of these sites require a listing fee, similar to traditional directories, but may be worth it. Think about your industry and do some Google'ing. That's often the best way to find authority sites in your niche. Develop a profile on the site and be sure to include a link to your website.

One additional idea to keep in mind is proper link building – I can't stress this enough. Vary your anchor text using your URL and brand name about 60 – 70% of the time when building one way links. Also, build links slowly over time. Using a service that builds links for you with adequate spacing is the key to long-term dominance of search engine result listings.

Social Media Sites

Unless you've been living under a rock for the last few years, it's hard to ignore the explosive growth of social media. It seems that every day existing social media sites are getting larger and new ones are cropping up all over the place. This popularity is driven by the viral nature of social media. You invite your friends, they invite their friends, and before you know it, the whole world is connected.

I've been participating in social media for a long time. A number of social media sites have come and gone over the years, but some continue to dominate the social media space. Facebook, Twitter, YouTube, Pinterest, LinkedIn, the list goes on. And Google is not hiding the fact that social actions weigh into their every-changing algorithm.

By now you know that I have a one-track mind. That's certainly true when it comes to social media and its impact on SEO. One must ask the question, "How can I use social media sites to improve the ranking of my own websites and blogs?" There are two answers to that question and they are very much aligned to what we've been talking about in this section. The answer is "links" and "rankings."

Social media links are created when you develop a profile on a social media website like Facebook. If you have a Facebook account it likely includes links of various kinds—links to books you're reading, products and websites you recommend, and hopefully links back to your website or blog. By the very nature of Facebook, it carries tremendous authority. If you are linking to your own website, it passes that authority back to you. When setting up your profile on Facebook, Twitter, Linkedin, YouTube, and other social media sites, you should always include at least one link back to your website and other digital assets.

Keep in mind that it's not only your links that provide value. In fact, what others are saying (in the form of inbound links, likes, retweets, etc.) carries a lot of weight too. If the social media universe is talking about and sharing information regarding particular websites, Google takes notice. When considering how to leverage social media for search engine optimization purposes, always be thinking about how simple it is to share your content across multiple networks. As we discussed in the amplifying content section, make it easy for others to share your content and link to your offers. Social media sharing has never been easier and the benefits can be directly correlated to search engine ranking success.

New studies come out on a weekly basis showing new correlations between social media and search engine rankings. The reality is there are many different ways online to learn about your brand or website. Today, one of the most popular is social media. If you haven't delved into the area of social media, you must. For those who want top organic rankings, social media is no longer a nice to have, it's a must-have.

Facebook

Let's begin with Facebook. Signing up and getting started with Facebook is very easy and you've probably been using a personal account for quite some time. If not, visit the home page and complete the basic information then click, "Sign Up." Once you register, confirm, and set up your profile, you'll be able to take advantage of everything Facebook has to offer. When registering, complete all aspects of your profile and seek guidance from friends who are currently using Facebook for tips and guidance on the numerous Facebook features. Learning what to do and how to do it from current users is definitely the quickest way to get up to speed.

Keep in mind that your profile name will be visible in Facebook, so choose your naming convention carefully. This is something you'll want to give some thought to. Don't worry though. In addition to setting up an account under your name, you'll also be able to create a company profile (Page) for your website, blog, or business use. This gives you added visibility and the opportunity to add links that point to your website. Additionally, you can post other links on your "Wall." Setting up a business page is helpful because it will rank, without much effort on your part, within a few days of being created. This is because Facebook as so much authority that Google has no choice but to show it in search results if properly optimized.

Proper optimization is simple. Fill out as much of your business profile/page as you can. This means taking the time to add all of your business information, add photos, update settings, etc. The more information you provide the better. The other thing you should be focused on is making regular updates to your page. The more active you are, the more weight your page receives. With more weight comes more online exposure. Take the time to do it right!

The true SEO value of Facebook is in building a network and asking others to post or share your links on their profile pages, wall, or on their own digital assets such as blogs and forums. Over time, your profile, and the links distributed by those in your network are what create SEO value. Many of those links will come from other business sites where your company is listed. These sites often ask for your Facebook page URL in addition to your website URL, it's that common. Don't miss this opportunity to heavily promote your business and generate quality inbound links to your site.

As individuals like your webpages and you build a following, you exponentially grow the potential value of your social media account. Just like the old adage, "always be selling," I like to say, "Always be sharing". Share all of your updates with followers and ask them to share with others. A number of tests completed by Moz and other leading search engine optimization firms have proven the positive impact of Facebook shares on search engine result placements. As such, always focus on getting your content "shared" versus "liked". Sharing does more for SEO.

Twitter

The concept of Twitter is still effective even though other sites are integrating their concept of micro-updates. After registering and setting up a profile, you create short posts of 280 characters or less including text, a link, and/or media. These posts are visible to everyone who is following you as well as those viewing a particular thread. Threads are visible using a hashtag. Hashtags are identified by the pound sign "#" and appear before a phrase (ex: #SEO). If I'm subscribed to "#SEO" for example, I'll be able to view anyone's Tweet that is followed with #SEO thanks to this hashtag feature.

Recent studies have shown a direct correlation between Twitter engagement and website popularity. Although many of my clients have focused predominantly on Facebook, I now stress the importance of Twitter in addition because of this data.

Using Twitter for SEO is a two-part process. The first part is to include a link to your website from your Twitter profile. After logging in to your profile, click on the "edit your profile link" and "Profile" from the top menu. You will see a location for your web address. Enter your URL there. Once you start building Twitter followers, and they link to your profile, this will improve the authority of this link.

The second way to use Twitter for SEO is to build a list of Twitter followers. You can do this by sharing your handle (example: @mfleischner) on your blog, in your marketing messages, on your website, email signature, and so on. Always focus on growing a targeted list of followers.

Many individuals set up automated following. That means if you follow them, they will follow you back. You can start following individuals of interest manually or use automated software to do so. Although I don't recommend this for everyone, if you are just starting out on Twitter, taking advantage of automated following is a great way to build a list quickly. Once you have a list of targeted followers, you can make them aware of valuable content and features available on your website. Always make your content valuable and easy share with others.

It's essential that you consider what type of content you'll deliver on Twitter. I've built a following of more than ten thousand people by giving helpful SEO-related strategies on a regular basis. Focus on your niche and "Tweet" about an area you know a lot about.

By exposing your brand, website, and targeted links to a growing audience, the likelihood of building inbound links and website popularity increases. If you're not tweeting yet, get started. It's an essential component of your SEO strategy and can feed other social media platforms via automatic updates.

Google My Business - Social

I have to admit, I was never a huge fan of Google+ which has likely become a distant memory for most of us. It was Google's attempt to win at social media but it never really caught on. At least not to the extent of Facebook, Instagram, or Youtube. You would think that because I know so much about Google I'd be excited to engage in their social venture to build a powerful social network. But the network was awkward and didn't really help promote me or my business effectively. The only redeeming quality was the SEO benefit.

As we discussed earlier, the search engine optimization benefit of any social media is really found in the profile itself and the sharing of your content. The same was true for Google. After their ill-fated attempt to make Google+ the next big thing, they threw in the towel, but not completely. Instead of abandoning social all together, they instead decided to integrate the concept of social, micro-content, into their Google My Business profiles.

This means that any business with a Google My Business profile, which should be everyone at this point, has the ability to create social posts on a regular basis. And you should. When you log into your Google My Business profile, look for "posts" on the left hand side. There you'll be able to draft and publish a post about your business. I recommend making 2x posts per week. Alternatively, if you're using software to schedule your posts like Hootsuite, you can develop and plan your posts to automatically post on specific days and times. Since Big Fin SEO has been making social contributions on our clients' GMB profiles, we've seen better rankings and improved engagement – so Google is clearly paying attention.

My recommendation is to post twice a week always including a link to your website or blog. I recommend sharing content from your actual site, driving people to a variety of website pages instead of your home page. This creates some link diversity and no doubt helps Google access key features of your website. The end result is more links pointing to your site, more traffic and engagement, resulting in improved rankings and exposure for your business.

Youtube

Have you published videos to Youtube? It is one of the largest sources of traffic on the planet and in integral part of organic search results. Video is one of the most effective ways to earn top rankings and produce value-added content that can supercharge your social media. Not only can video generate inbound links, but as a digital asset it can often appear directly in search results. Video is easy to optimize and has a high click-through rate.

Creating and distributing videos is easier than ever thanks to mobile phones and portable devices with amazing cameras. Leveraging the Youtube platform needs to be an integral part of your SEO strategy. Begin by creating an account on Youtube that's optimized around your website's theme. Once you register, you'll have a number of options available to you.

Click on your username and select "Account." If you click on "Profile Setup" in the left margin, you'll see a place to enter your URL. In addition, each time you upload an optimized video, you can enter a proper title and description. If you've never produced a video before, don't worry. Creating videos for SEO purposes is easier than ever and can be outsourced using vendors on *UpWork* or related websites.

When you upload a video to Youtube, you'll have the opportunity to provide a title and description. Your title should include your target keyword, preferably towards the beginning, just like writing a title tag for meta data. When you write descriptions for your video, start with a URL that appears in the beginning. This helps it show in search results, helping promote your site and generating direct traffic.

Optimizing your video properly on Youtube not only ensures good visibility on the Youtube platform itself but also supports visibility on Google search results. Optimizing your video properly is essential for increasing the likelihood of having it appear in Google's universal search results and requires just a few basic guidelines. To optimize your video, follow these guidelines:

- Use your keyword phrases in the audio (first 25 words) portion of your video. That's right it's highly likely that Google is using audio keywords to help rank videos appropriately.

- List your keywords in the video title, description, and keywords (at least twice) when submitting your video.

- Make sure your video title is optimized for your keyword.

- Generate a four paragraph description that includes your keyword in each.

- Add your "keywords" to the video in the keyword box provided.

- Make your video accessible to all viewers.

- Add a location for your video.

- Generate views and shares of your video by posting on social media, especially Google My Business, Facebook, and Twitter.

- Develop a video channel that includes more than one video.

- Make your videos longer than 1 minute in length.

- Get your videos indexed by building links to them.

One of the best ways to promote your video and, therefore, your link, is to tell others about it. Youtube has a subscribe option allowing users to access all the videos you produce and post to Youtube. Once you learn more about Youtube and establish your own "channel" (a collection of videos) individuals can subscribe, receiving a notification each time you post a new video.

One of the most important aspects for optimization is the potential interaction of those viewing your videos. After viewing your content, visitors can "like" your video or leave a comment. Always encourage your audience to "Like" and rate your videos. One effective method for doing so is the use of captions. Youtube makes it very easy to add captions to your video that can be used to encourage interaction among those watching your video.

There are many factors that go into optimizing your Youtube video. However, one thing we know for certain is that Youtube videos are ranked by the number of Subscribers, "Likes," and comments. Whenever you produce a video, promote the video by sharing with your list and embedding in your website or blog. Encourage users to like the video and leave comments. This can help your ranking in Youtube and may encourage third-party websites to embed the video directly into their content. Sharing and embedding videos means more links to the video itself, which in turn creates more link juice. Over time the number and quality of links pointing to your site through your Youtube link gain authority which helps your rankings.

If you've never created a Youtube video, don't despair. There is a great deal of quality video on Youtube and Vimeo that show you simple ways of creating professional looking videos. Spend some time learning the art of video making or just use your mobile device. Publishing videos is relatively easy and video production doesn't need to be complicated. In fact, many of my videos are simply a minute of video shot using my mobile phone. As long as your content is meaningful, you're using keywords in your audio, optimizing your title, description and keywords when uploading it, you are starting to generate positive SEO value. Once you know how to produce a simple video, you can fuel your link-building efforts in a powerful way by posting and encouraging social interaction.

Another thing to keep in mind is that most people watch video with the sound off. When making your video, always include captions so individuals can watch with the sound off. When uploading videos to different social channels, many will auto-generate captions for your video. But don't assume they're correct. Always review an edit your captions to improve their readability.

Once you've published your video on Youtube or other social media channels, it's important to let others where they can find you – on Facebook, Twitter, etc. Use social sharing tools to create share buttons on your website, blog, and other content where your videos can be found. This makes it easy for website visitors to follow you on all of your social media channels. Keep in mind that today it's not just about your content, it's how popular your content is among your target audience. So focus on sharing it whenever and wherever you can.

Over time, as more and more browsers engage with your content (videos in particular), the number and quantity of social connections will continue to increase. These follows serve as inbound links to your content, website, or web page, helping to boost Google SERPs. When you begin using social as a way to expand your online footprint, you will improve rankings and more importantly the number of results that appear in search results.

Regardless of which social media platform you favor, having a presence on the most popular ones, which do change over time, is essential for the development of third-party links to your website. They add value and produce positive social signals that Google relies on to rank websites and related content. If you aren't actively engaged with social media, get started today. Consider using a social media management tool like Hootsuite to automate posts across all of your social media accounts. The sooner you become active with social media the faster you build online authority.

If would like to determine the availability for you or your company name on social media channels, be sure to check out Knowem. The site lets you crawl hundreds of sites to check for profile availability around a specific name. Taking the time to claim your profile on these sites is also a great way to build quality inbound links to your website.

In addition to Facebook, Twitter, and Google, look to expand onto other social media sites aligned with your business. For example, if you have a bakery, you probably want to share some of those delicious cakes on Instagram and Pinterest. If you are a real estate developer and target other commercial businesses, you probably want to focus on LinkedIn. My recommendation is to start with Facebook, Twitter, and Google, and go from there. When you do, you'll have a solid social media foundation.

The names of the dominant social media sites will change over time, but the strategy remains sound. Focus on high authority social media sites that allow you to expand your online presence and connect with your target audience. Make it easy for potential users to find and follow you on social media. This is work that can be done easily and consistently to build website authority.

Press Releases

One of the best strategies I've used to get my link distributed on hundreds of authority websites, almost overnight, is through press release distribution. Even though the public relations community has practically dismissed the use of the old fashioned press release, it still remains a powerful SEO tool – especially in this age of social media and Google's constant demand for quality content. The way this technique works is by distributing a press release—an announcement of news related to your website—containing links back to your website. Now you might be saying, "Hey, I'm not in public relations and I know nothing about press releases." That's OK; you can use the press release resource I've listed at myseomadesimple.com/resources and distribute a simple release to media outlets across the web containing links back to your website.

Now that Google displays universal and customized search results, press releases and other forms of digital media appear on page one of search results if aligned to specific search queries. In addition to using press releases to build inbound links to your website (from the press release sites and websites that pick up your release), you can also often get page one listings for a brief time if your release is newsworthy and unique.

I've used press releases for a long time to help with search engine ranking and promote affiliate web pages with a high degree of success. I needed to spin my releases and redistribute, but for a time it was very effective for driving traffic and conversions. When researching your keyword, take notice of the press release sites that appear on page one or two of the SERPs. Register for those sites and distribute your own releases through the same channels. Simple? Yes. Effective? Yes. Give it a try and you'll see why press releases are a great tool for improving your search engine rankings and website traffic!

Before distributing a release, consider the different types of releases you can create. The most valuable press releases are newsworthy and can stand on their own. When you share actual news, the likelihood of that information getting picked up by online news outlets and distributed to hundreds or even thousands of sites can quickly become a reality.

In my opinion the best way to create news is through an online poll or survey. Here are a couple of suggestions for creating a poll that is newsworthy and supports the press release strategy.

Option 1: If you're starting from scratch I recommend adding a poll question to your blog or social media account The only reason I suggest adding it to your blog or social media versus your website is they usually offer tools like online polling with a single click. If you haven't started a blog yet, take five minutes to create one on your website using a tool like Wordpress.

Option 2: If you have your own list of opt-in e-mails, use a tool like SurveyMonkey to develop a short survey and distribute. The survey will be the best $20 you ever spend. You can find more information on this survey solution at http://SurveyMonkey.com. As always, you can choose any survey solution as long as you have a predetermined list you can send it to. I would suggest leaving your poll or survey open until you've gotten at least one hundred responses. Preferably, you should target around 250, but one hundred should suffice for your first release. Once you've completed your first survey and written your press release, you can select an online press release distribution service. A variety of sources can distribute your press release and usually charge between $1 and $250.

Keep in mind that a press release is any bit of information that your prospective market would find of interest or value. For example, I've distributed releases when I launched my website and each time I collected information from an online poll. You could also distribute a press release each time you add a new feature to your site that delivers value or is unique to the market you serve.

The primary purpose of your press release is to build links to your website. Although I've used this strategy to achieve page one rankings for a short time, the actual value is created when other sites link to your release, which in turn is linking to your own website or blog. This is what Google needs to recognize and rank your website properly. As such, you want to select a distribution option where *your link is active and you can specify the link text.* If the press release distribution option doesn't include an active link, meaning a link to your website, select a different option or service.

I've used PRWeb for distribution services with my own press releases. However, PRWeb can get a bit pricey especially if using their SEO optimized release option. If you're just starting out and don't have the budget for a top-notch service, I recommend using PR-Inside or Newswire.com. They offer less distribution, but you can choose a more affordable option that lets you embed a link and specify anchor text. The key is to see which press release sites are already ranking in search results for your desired keyword phrases. Always make sure to use those sites which are currently generating listings on page one of Google search results.

Once distributed, give your release a few days to be picked up by the media and media outlets. The beauty of the press release is that "good news travels fast." After receiving initial media pickup, your release continues to be distributed for days and weeks to come. You can accelerate this process by bookmarking the release or sharing via social media. The press release, if newsworthy, is a fantastic tool for developing Google-friendly links.

Forum and Community Marketing

The Internet is an amazing place. If you have a question, about anything, you can usually find the answer online. This is especially true when it comes to search engine optimization, pay-per-click, and other forms of online marketing. In fact, when searching for an answer to a question via Google or any search engine, you're bound to find a listing for a blog post or forum. Forums, which are less popular today than they once were, are essentially online communities where similar minded people share ideas, ask questions, and answer them too. I guess you could say that forums were the precursor to social media communities.

Forums have been around a long time. Although they've lost steam in the last few years, there are still many forums online, especially in particular niches. Many of these forums have tens of thousands of members. These communities are large and provide the type of interaction you need to answer any question on a particular topic. How can you use forums to improve your rankings? The answer is simple. You can use forums to generate inbound links to your websites and blogs. The question of how to do this effectively is what we are focusing on.

The first step in any link-building initiative is to find a relevant forum and start posting. You can begin by doing a Google search forums I your niche. There are a few things that you need to consider in relation to forums:

- Is the forum related to your niche?

- Is the forum well established? Is it new or has it existed for some time?

- Does the forum have a good authority

- Does the forum seem active?

- Does the forum allow links in your signature? Are the links "do follow" links?

After researching possible forums and creating a list of at least three that meet your criteria, it's time to register and start posting. Before you post there are a few things you'll need to take care of. The first is to register for the forum accepting the terms and conditions. This is a very simple process that may require a valid email and clicking on a confirmation link. Once complete, you can log into the forum and visit your control panel.

The control panel is the place on the forum where you can set up your preferences and your forum signature. All forums have a control panel which may be labeled as the "CP" or "Profile." This is the area where you control how your forum signature, what shows beneath each post, will appear. Keep in mind that many forums require you to make ten full posts before allowing your signature to show. This is due to the fact that more and more people are using forums to build third-party links to their websites, blogs, and affiliate offers.

Set up your signature to include a link to your website using a keyword phrase or website URL as your anchor text. Many signatures allow up to three links but I would limit your signature to only two. Once your signature is set up, it's time to start posting. Always check the box that says "display my signature" if available.

To make the most of your forum posting, find threads (questions and responses) about a topic on which you can comment. Having my own forum, I know that many of the posts can be of poor quality. When they are, moderators may delete them. If you're going to leave a comment on a forum, make sure it's a good one. The more valuable your comments, the more staying power they'll have. Additionally, a number of forums have integrated social media opportunities. This means that if your question or response is of high quality, others may use social bookmarks to identify them or share via social media outlets like Twitter and Facebook. Similar to blog commenting, forum posts should be relevant, meaningful, and valuable. This gives your signature links the "link juice" you want.

Always pace your forum posting. The goal is to find a few highly relevant forums that you or a support person can actively contribute to on a monthly basis. I used to spend a lot of time in forums but found that forum posting—although extremely valuable—can be very time consuming as well. A few forum-posting tools out there can aid in making posts, but manual submissions are still the most powerful and require a little work.

Later in this guide I share some of my outsourcing strategies. Forum posting is a repetitive task others can do for you. Outsourcing something like forum posting provides a really good return on your investment when considering the trade-off between time and money. My recommendation is to do the research, set up your profiles and make the initial posts on the most popular niche forums. Once you've completed that work you are in a great position to outsource forum posting activities.

Caution: A lot of people assume that any time they want to promote a different website or change a signature for future posts they can simply log into their forum control panel and change their signature. The assumption is that changing their signature only affects future posts. This is often not the case. Changing your signature may impact all existing posts already submitted on the forum. If you want to build links to additional web pages, it may be necessary to create multiple accounts so you can have unique signatures linking to multiple websites. Again, it's all about the quality of inbound links to your website and forums are just another resource you can use to develop quality in-bound links.

Aged Domains

Another technique, ideal for authority link building, and mentioned previously, is the use of an Aged Domain. Personally I've found the use of aged domains to be very helpful from an SEO perspective. I could probably write an entire book on how to choose and leverage an aged domain so I'm simply going to point you in the right direction here. An aged domain is one that was established some time ago and may even have some traffic coming to it. You can search for and buy aged domains using GoDaddy or Sedo.com. If you purchase an aged domain that already has a portion of your primary keyword phrase included, the better. This can give you a jump start when launching your website because it has been indexed by Google, likely has inbound links, and may currently rank for the keywords for which you're trying to optimize.

There are a number of people who make a living out of selling or repurposing aged domains. These individual also have resources to help them keep the content on those sites current. Keep in mind that even if you purchase an aged domain, you'll need to optimize it and continually make updates and promote among social channels. If you don't have the bandwidth for this, focus on the other strategies provided. If you're willing to give it a go, definitely focus on aged domains that have some authority – that's the benefit of buying them. And be sure to drop links on the sites or redirect them to your target website.

The final way to think about aged domains is picking up a whole other website at low cost. In addition to Sedo.com, I recommend checking out Flippa, where you can buy complete websites. Buying an aged domain or website is a great way to leverage established authority to help your website, blogs, and other digital assets increase in authority and rankings.

Give People a Reason to Link to Your Website

One of the best ways to attract one-way links to your website and improve website authority to improve rankings is by promoting free content via your own website or blog. This may include anything of value such as news or articles, white papers, free tools, and so on. Using this idea of developing value-added content is aligned with the link-building strategy we've been discussing. Using this strategy, you are creating valuable content and subscribing to that old adage, "If you build it, they will come." It might sound cliché, but thanks to social media and the web, you can attract users to your website (and links) by having something of value to offer. If you provide something of sufficient quality, other websites will start linking to you, giving one-way links that can dramatically improve your search engine results.

Developing article collections that provide a wealth of information to website browsers seeking information in your niche is a great start. Assuming you have a site related to your niche, you can easily start writing about important topics or solicit guest posts from others in your niche.

I've also seen a lot of success with lite applications like an online calculator or tool that evaluates or scans a particular website in some manner. If you have an idea for a useful tool, make your way over to Upwork or similar freelance site and see what it would cost to build and add to your website. By having valuable content, you'll attract more and more links.

Another suggestion is the creation of a small promotional ebook or Top 10 List. If you've ever downloaded a book electronically from the Web, you already have experience with ebooks and quality content. When users know they can get something, even a small promotional ebook for free, they tell others. This creates a "viral" effect that is great for attracting one-way links.

If you can create an ebook of your own or exclusive list, regardless of its length, develop it in Word and save it out as a PDF. As a last step, post it on your website and make it easily available for individuals to access. Be sure to include your site information in the footer of the content and encourage people to share it by linking back to your site. If you need help with your ebook, Top 10 list, or exclusive content, consider leveraging work others have done. The best way to do this is to search for PLR-related materials. PLR stands for *private label rights*, and you can often "buy" the rights to completed ebooks, how-to manuals, and the like, for little or no money.

The next step is to offer these PLR materials on your website for free. Before long, others will be linking to you because you're providing something of value. Just make sure they are linking in the right way and you're doing what you can to let others know that content is available. On your web page, encourage people to link to your resources and provide them with the proper link text (e.g., If you'd like to link to us, please use the following html code: <a href="http://www.yoursitename.com" title="your keyword phrase" rel="dofollow">Your keyword phrase</a>).

As you proactively develop links for your website, start creating and publishing content on your own website that others in your niche find valuable. By doing so, you accelerate link development and continually enhance your link profile.

As I mentioned at the start of this section, off-page optimization is the most important factor for improving Google SERPs for your websites, blogs, images, and any asset appearing in search results. Use the *SEO Made Simple* techniques to build quality links to your website and watch your search engine rankings soar!

All of these off-page optimization techniques, when applied consistently over time, significantly improve Google SERPs and results on other major search engines. After implementing the various off-page optimization methods we've covered, select those you are most comfortable with and apply them on a regular basis.

Now that you understand the techniques for effective search engine optimization, it's time to think about getting it all done. In the next section I'm going to share my personal experiences with outsourcing and how to find and efficient, inexpensive resource to help you achieve search engine dominance.

Outsourcing

After many years of creating content, optimizing websites, and spending countless hours building links to websites and blogs, a good friend of mine turned me on the concept of outsourcing. Personally, I never really trusted anyone with my web properties or SEO and still tread lightly. However, over the past couple of years I have found a number of outsourcing partners that I use to support the optimization of my websites and take on the more mundane SEO tasks I need to do on a regular basis – and so can you.

The concept of outsourcing is simple. Find other people to do repetitive or time-consuming tasks at a low cost. While they are focusing on "getting it done," you can focus on new projects, revenue-generating activities, and other work.

I used to think that outsourcing was only for large companies. To be honest I had a number of misconceptions about outsourcing and the types of individuals that support outsourcing-related jobs. The reality is that you can find a number of highly qualified, intelligent individuals who are willing to complete work at a much lower cost than expected thanks to our global economy. I've used freelancers in India, Sweden, the Philippines, and other places across the globe for programming, link building, and administrative tasks.

Whether you're working on a single website or twenty, I recommend learning more about the opportunity to outsource specific tasks. There are a variety of resources that allow you to find just the right person to support your SEO. My personal favorite is Upwork. There are many others available such as Freelancer.com, Fiverr, etc. or those like 99Designs that focus primarily on design. So find the site that will meet your most immediate and long-term demands.

Here's how outsourcing for a typical SEO project might work. You begin by defining tasks that you want to complete on a daily, weekly, or monthly basis. Spend some time thinking about what you can handle on your own and what you can give to someone else. Focus on where your time is best spent. What should you be paying someone else do versus doing yourself? By spending time up front to determine which tasks should be outsourced and those you can handle on your own, you are more likely to choose the right outsource partner.

As an example, let's say that you want to outsource forum posting or blog posting for your SEO campaign. The first thing you have to do is ask yourself how effective an outsourcing partner can be with either of these tasks. For me, I'd say that forum posting is probably easier for an international person than blog posting. This is because blog commenting requires an individual to read a blog post (in a language they understand), find an entry to comment on, and write a well-articulated response in the appropriate language. This increases your chances of having a comment "stick" and therefore requires some level of expertise. Forum posting, from my perspective, requires some of the same skills as blog commenting, but not always. I could likely find dozens of IT-related blogs that talk about programming languages and anyone with a little HTML or php experience could write a post or comment on a thread. Seek out an outsource partner who has experience with forum posting in general and specific content knowledge to be effective.

While your freelancer is doing the heavy lifting on specific SEO tasks, you can focus on other high-value SEO tactics. This may include niche-specific article writing or article spinning which requires a native speaker and someone with a good grasp of the subject matter. Article writing, spinning, and distribution are best done "in house" but I've seen some SEO professionals outsource this successfully as well. Between outsourcing and the use of semi-automated tools you can often reduce the time it takes to complete optimization activities quite substantially.

Once you've created a list of tasks you want to outsource, it's time to find a suitable provider. As noted earlier, Upwork provides access to a significant number of potential freelancers and technology companies who can help you with anything SEO or programming related. If you have programming needs that are sufficient in scale, I recommend testing a variety of vendors. You can post a project and have multiple providers bid on your job, read through reviews, samples of work, etc. to help determine which vendor can best meet your needs. You may want to consider breaking your larger project into smaller ones until you can find the developer that's right for you.

Overall I've had a very positive experience with Upwork and the providers available through their network. That doesn't necessarily guarantee success however. My advice is to approach the concept of outsourcing as a work in progress. Keep experimenting with different vendors until you find the perfect match. Once you select a provider, set up project milestones – key deliverables that must be accomplished by certain dates in exchange for payment. A great feature of freelance platforms is the ability to pay your vendor upon completion of each milestone. This keeps everyone honest and your project moving forward. As you start working with outsourcers, record which ones you like and which ones you'd never use again. In time you'll have a short list of affordable vendors you can use for virtually anything web related.

If you are looking for freelancers who can support your search engine optimization activities like link building, article writing, blogging, etc., I recommend using a freelancer platform with a clear understanding of what you need done, by when, and at what price. These platforms offers a robust search that helps you narrow down candidates rather quickly. Contact the individuals you are considering for services and ask them to do a small assignment for you. If they're successful, consider hiring them on a regular basis. Make them feel like part of your team and remember they can't read your mind. Be very specific with regard to the tasks you want accomplished and your greatly improve the chances of a positive outcome. This type of management takes some work and usually a bit of effort up front but can page huge dividends quickly. Once you find a good freelancer for a given task, it lightens your burden and increases productivity as much as ten-fold. Over time, experiment with additional techniques that could possibly move the needle for you on search results.

As your business grows and you gain more experience with SEO, I highly recommend taking advantage of outsourcing. I have found qualified programmers for $8-$20/hr. and individuals to help with SEO tasks for as little as $5-$10/hr. Not only is the quality of work excellent, but affordable too. This allows me to focus on bigger and better projects while having more time to spend with family and friends—a real priority in my life.

Caution: Automated Tools, Shortcuts, and Other SEO Blunders!

Now that I've shared the link-building methods I've used to successfully achieve top search engine rankings, and build a number of online businesses, I thought I'd cover some of the do's and do not's you should consider when implementing any search engine optimization program.

For starters, let me remind you that search engine optimization is a marathon not a sprint. This is something I've shared with all of our clients who either expect instant results or don't have a full grasp on how search engine optimization works.

If you want page one listings in twenty-four hours, I can do that for you. All I would need to do is find a keyword phrase that isn't all that competitive and shows listings for press releases, articles, or social media on page one of Google. Then I'd put a link on my high authority blog with the keyword in the title or send out a press release from a site that already displays a result on page one. And like clockwork, you'd see the target site listed on the first page of Google. But what's the point? Once indexed, the corresponding listing will be there for a few hours at best only to vanish as quickly as it arrived. SEO is not about creating a flash in the pan but rather applying search engine optimization best practices that result in top rankings that last. If you can accomplish that goal for your business, everyone wins.

To get to the top of the SERPs, you must start with on page optimization and pace your link-building efforts. In the next section, I'll actually show you how to do this with a step-by-step optimization framework. Remember, build links too quickly and you'll get penalized. Build them methodically over time, and in the right way, and you'll achieve lasting results. Always keep the long-term in mind when it comes to SEO. I can tell you from years of SEO experience that when you start an active link-building campaign you may experience what's known as the "Google Dance." This is when you see your results shoot up one day, disappear the next, and bounce from position to position over a short period of time. This is actually a good sign. It means that Google is acknowledging your link-building activity and trying to award your site with an appropriate search position. Also remember that it's common to see little movement during the first few weeks or months of a link building campaign. Even if you don't see movement right away, stay the course. Upward movement of search position can happen steadily over time if you apply enough effort. Often times, you have to prime the pump before you see results much like an old watering hole. Keep the faith in the "made simple" methodology because it works. Optimizing your web pages and building quality inbound links produces lasting results.

The other area to consider is link diversity. More often than not, you are going to find one link-building technique that you prefer above all others. This is natural and occurs with almost everyone. Nonetheless, you have to remember that Google is not just looking for inbound links; they are also looking at link diversity. You need to focus on attracting links of all kinds, not just a specific kind. Articles, blogs, forums, etc. all matter. Always seek to build a diverse set of inbound links from a variety of sources (.com, .edu, .net, etc.) versus putting all your eggs in one basket. If you were to focus on a single link type and Google changed their algorithm and devalued those links, your SEO efforts would become meaningless. Spread the risk and show Google that sites of all kinds are linking to your online resources.

One area that you should always be cautious of is full SEO automation. As mentioned previously, I've experimented with link building automation tools, and unless used properly and responsibly, they will have a detrimental impact on your rankings. Don't fall prey to the dozens of vendors who promise overnight rankings or instant results – they don't exist. I confess that I do use a few automated tools myself but in a very limited way to help manage the dozens of websites and blogs I'm optimizing for at any given moment. However, none of these tools can handle 100% of the work.

Once you start with a technically optimized website (on page optimization), link building becomes one of the most important things you'll need to do for optimization but is probably the place where most people go wrong. When building links, keep in mind the same adage I've mentioned throughout this guide, *slow and steady win the race*. Additionally place a good deal of focus on your link profile, specifically anchor text. Review the earlier section in this book on anchor text again and again. You should use your URL and brand-name as anchor text a good deal of the time – as much as 50% - when link building. This is what Google considers to be natural as opposed to using the same anchor text over and over again. Being domain and brand focused with anchor text is the most effective link building strategy you can have.

The final area of caution is trying to be a lone ranger. When I started in SEO there wasn't much of an SEO community. Today, tens of thousands of people either make a living with search engine optimization or at least participate in SEO-related discussions on a regular basis. I encourage you to reach out to others in the community via forums and other online resources to ask questions and join the discussion.

Also, keep in mind that search engine optimization is literally changing by the day. Through core Google updates, changes in the search engine landscape, and new ways to market and promote digital assets, it's important to stay on top of SEO or find a partner (freelancer, agency, etc.) who continually makes tweaks to your website and strategy, taking advantage of the latest and greatest SEO factors.

Search engine optimization has faced many significant changes over the last decade but remains as one of the best, and most important ways to grow your business.

Section Two Summary

Here's what you should take away from this section about off-page optimization:

- ✓ Off-page optimization is your key to Google success.

- ✓ Your success on Google is based on which websites are linking to you and how they link to you.

- ✓ Link quality is essential for improving SERPs.

- ✓ When engaging in a reciprocal link, make sure that the website that is providing a link back to you has an equal or greater authority rating. This is important for maintaining a favorable Google balance.

- ✓ There are essentially three types of links: one-way, reciprocal, and three-way linking. One-way links, especially if they are from a page with a high authority, are the best.

- ✓ The most effective way to identify the right sites to get links from is to identify who is linking to your competition. You can do this by using search engine optimization software or by using major search engines.

- ✓ Sources for identifying inbound links to competitors include Google and SEO tools like Open Site Explorer.

- ✓ Use a variety of link text when link building with greater utilization of your domain name (URL) and brand name.

- ✓ Include a variety of keywords and/or keyword phrases in your link text about 30% or more of the time.

- ✓ When link building, remember that quality attracts quality.

- ✓ Be persistent, take massive action, pace yourself, and the links will come.

- ✓ Build your inbound links with the help of:
  - ○ content marketing

- link exchanges/link requests
- local directory submissions
- social media sites
- blogging
- press releases
- forum marketing
- authority links
- aged domains

✓ Give people a reason to link to your website.

✓ Use outsourcing to free up your time and complete repetitive tasks.

✓ Be careful with some automated link building tools as they can negatively impact your website ranking unless used properly.

✓ Get involved with the SEO community through forums and news feeds.

Section 3

Research to Practice

Developing a Game Plan

One of the most valuable lessons I've learned in the last decade that I've been doing SEO is having a game plan. It's not enough to possess the knowledge you must apply it regularly to have the results you desire.

In an effort to simplify the game plan and help you succeed, this chapter spells out the plan for applying the techniques you've learned. The good news is that getting started is easy to do and I'm personally taking the guesswork out of this entire process by laying out the plan to get you started.

On-page Optimization

Begin with keyword research. This is one of the most important things you can do to amplify your organic results. By finding the most targeted, highly trafficked keywords with the least amount of organic traffic, you can quickly and dramatically improve organic rankings. With improved rankings comes more website traffic and sales. Don't short change yourself by skipping keyword research. For details, re-read the section on keyword research and develop a list of 10 – 20 target keyword phrases and consider long-tail keywords for best results.

Once you've done your keyword research, begin with on-page optimization. If you want the quickest and easiest path to on-page optimization, sign up for a free crawl with MOZ or SEMrush. Let the technology crawl your website and return "errors" based on SEO best practices. I have used, and continue to use, both of these services to save hours of time evaluating websites. Once you receive an SEO optimization report, slowly and methodically begin making changes to your site focusing on your most important keywords. By eliminating crawl errors, improving site accessibility, and remediating all on-page issues, you'll make a significant and positive impact on organic results. Keep in mind that your priority should be optimizing your home page and top-level pages, followed by your secondary pages.

If there are optimizations you're not able to implement, including those requiring code changes, find a freelancer to do the work for you. Use a site like *UpWork* to find a qualified freelancer who knows something about SEO and the platform your website is hosted on. You can find an expert in pretty much anything so it doesn't really matter what platform you're using, whether it's a custom CMS or WordPress site.

After changes have been implemented, run another SEO report. If you subscribe to Moz or SEMrush, you can set up monthly or weekly crawl reports to ensure that changes have addressed the most salient SEO factors. If SEO software isn't in your budget, consider paying for a single website crawl or signing up for a month and then cancelling. Remember, it's not enough to simply identify SEO issues, you need to address them and do a final review to ensure everything has been properly optimized. On a go forward basis, as you build additional pages, implement best practices you have learned from *SEO Made Simple* and the software program you're using to crawl your website on an ongoing basis. This ensures compliance with best practices and gives website pages the best chances of attaining top organic placements.

Google Connection

After you've completed your on-page changes, the next step is get your site re-indexed and connected with Google. Here are two very easy and powerful ways to get started.

1. **Sign up for Google My Business**. It takes about 5 minutes to sign up and register your company/site with Google. As you add information about your website or business to your *Google My Business* profile, fill out as much information as possible and post regularly. The more information you provide, the more Google will want to show you in search results.

2. **Sign up for Google Console.** Once registered, Google will ask you to verify your account. If you are not clear on verification methods, watch a YouTube video on how to do so or hire a freelancer. After verification, upload an xml-sitemap to your Google Webmasters Account. You can create an xml-sitemap for free at xml-sitemaps.com. It's incredibly easy to do so dive right in.

By submitting your business and/or website to *Google My Business*, registering for *Google Webmaster Tools*, and uploading your sitemap, you're 70% ahead of the majority of website owners when it comes to optimization. The reason I encourage the "Google Connection" after implementing on-site changes is because Google will be crawling an optimized website as opposed to one filled with errors. This provides a higher trust ranking and therefore improved search results.

Now that you've got all of the on-page optimization and Google notifications out of the way, it's time to start with content creation. By developing targeted, value-added content, we will be building up website authority and developing more inbound link opportunities.

Editorial Calendar

Begin your content develop program by creating and Editorial Calendar. Simply thinking through the needs and preferences of your market, and the types of information that are most valuable to them can eliminate hard work that goes unanswered. When you are producing content that matters, people will engage, interact, and share. These are the measures of an effective content development program.

About 70 – 80% of your content should be evergreen, the rest seasonal. Evergreen content can be produced once and remains relevant for years to come. Develop a topic for each month and then break it down into a couple pieces of evergreen content and then one or more seasonal pieces – targeting long tail keywords. An example of this from my perspective would be a marketer creating evergreen content regarding branding but in the same month (assuming it's the holiday season), adding something like, how to avoid shopping cart abandonment during the holidays. As you produce more content, you'll learn a lot about what subjects resonate with your audience and how to create messages that consumers engage with.

The next step is to package and post your content. Begin by publishing content on your website first whenever possible. Think about ways to take one piece of content and leverage it by using different types of media. For example, if you write and article, can you repackage as a quick video? How about a Power Point presentation? Perhaps a PDF summary of what you've written? Today's leading webmasters are able to take a single piece of content and re-package it in multiple ways. By learning to do so, you can originate less content but produce more digital assets for your website and distribution.

Once you've produced new content, the next step is to distribute it. Let's assume for a moment that you've produced new content, posted it on your site, and optimized it (keyword in file name, meta data, body copy, etc.). Now what? Well, let's start with social media. Assuming you've registered and optimized your profile on Facebook and Twitter, share your content on those channels, pointing back to the content's location on your own website. Also, integrate AddThis share buttons on your site near the top of your content so visitors who do consume it can share with others. Always make sure to share your content on Google My Business in addition to other popular social media channels. This ensures a Google crawl and indexing of your content.

Do this consistently for the next few months. Even if you're only producing a couple pieces of content: new web page, blog post, uploading images, videos, PDFs, slides, it's essential to do this on a consistent basis. Get in the habit of sharing across social media channels and encouraging others to share, repost, and engage with. After a few months, consider outsourcing this process but always focus on quality, original content that's well optimized and based on your editorial calendar.

Now that you've optimized your site and begun producing content, it's time to start building some links.

Link-Building Process

After you've created a strong foundation for your site through keyword research and on page optimization, and established yourself with Google by registering for *Google My Places*, *Google Console*, and building some valuable content for distribution, the next and final step is to begin a link building process slowly over time.

Even after spending days in workshops teaching people on-page optimization skills, there's always an added interest and desire for more information on how to tackle link building. I don't know why this has such an appeal, but it has always been a focal point for those learning the art of search engine optimization.

Based on the information you've read so far, you understand the importance of slow and steady link building. In fact, link-building cowboys are out there every day trying to get hundreds or thousands of links to their sites through services and shortcuts only to find that Google slaps them with a big penalty—setting their SEO back weeks or even months.

I've experimented with tons of paid link building services to support my search engine optimization efforts. Most of the time they either can't deliver what's promised or worse yet, have a negative impact on search results (ex: website submission services). To help manage the workload, I've used freelancers to help with the manual process of building quality inbound links slowly over time. This includes key directories and resource sites as well as niche sites focused on my particular client industries.

In this section I'm going to reveal the exact link-building system I've applied to achieve number one rankings for many of my websites and blogs. The first place to being is by focusing on your competition. No fancy software is needed, although using a tool like *Link Explorer* can greatly minimize the time and effort required to complete this task.

Begin by identifying the websites ranking in the first, second, and third spots of search results for one of your target keywords. The next step is to see who is linking to these top ranked sites. You can use an automated tool like Link Explorer, or the "link: www.example.com" command in a Google search box. Once you've aggregated your list of target web sites, and prioritized based on those with the most authority, visit each one to see if you can acquire a link to your own website. To see which sites have the greatest authority, use and SEO tool or browser plugin that shows you site authority, strength, or number of inbound links. You obviously want to target the most authoritative sites for link building purposes.

Keep in mind that it's virtually impossible to get a link on *every* site that your competitors have received links from. This is due to many factors including the reality they may own some of those sites. But don't despair. Work to acquire links from as many of the websites you've identified as you can. This may require outreach to the site owner, a guest article or post, maybe even a comment on their blog or in their community. Spend some time or hire a freelancer to research these authoritative sites and develop a strategy for obtaining a link – this increases your chances of success. This link building methodology provides a strong foundation for improving your rankings and beginning a regular link building process.

The "modeling" strategy we just described here is one of the most powerful and should command a good deal of your focus. By targeting the sites giving your competitors a boost you simultaneously improve your rankings while diminishing the value of their inbound links. After exhausting your target list of sites for strategic link building, it's time to implement your monthly link building program. And it all begins with a very simple spreadsheet.

Ongoing Link Building

Remember I said we would create a link building plan for you? Well, having a formula to follow for link building is the best and easiest way to build website authority over the long term. You want staying power. The best way to do so is applying a slow, steady, and consistent approach to acquiring links. Here's a snapshot of your plan.

Site Name - Month		
Task	Date	Initials
2 - 5 articles published to website/blog	MM/DD/YY	
2 - 4 blog submissions/comments	MM/DD/YY	
5 forum submissions	MM/DD/YY	
10 authority profile submissions	MM/DD/YY	
1 press releases	MM/DD/YY	
30 social media posts	MM/DD/YY	
1 video uploads	MM/DD/YY	
3 local search engine profiles	MM/DD/YY	

From my perspective, link building is a monthly process that you can effectively manage. Build links too quickly and you'll be penalized or perhaps achieve top rankings for only a short while (e.g., press releases). Build links too slowly and your competition may outrank you. Striking the perfect balance takes some experience and experimentation but is well within reach. I've spent a decade creating a link-building process that produces consistent results and simplified for you in this section. The only variable is the competitiveness of your niche, which impacts the rate of link building, and target link acquisition websites.

Recently I completed an SEO job for a well-known trucking company who wanted top rankings for a particular keyword phrase. This competitive phrase got nearly thirty thousand searches a month and had some very stiff competition. Although the company knew it would take a long time to achieve results they understood the value in achieving a top ranking for this term and decided to move forward. We applied the necessary SEO techniques and got the result they were looking for—but it took almost nine months. This is because the term was very competitive and other sites that were in the top positions had been there for a very long time. This is why doing the keyword research up-front, to find less competitive terms, is so important. Keep in mind that long tail keywords, those including 3 or more words, are easier to rank for and more aligned with how people actually search for things.

Once you have developed a website or blog, identified the keyword phrases you want to rank well for, and implemented on-page optimization techniques we've shared in this guide, the next step is to have a link-building plan to apply on a regular basis. After developing a comprehensive list of sites linking into the top few results for the keyword phrase you're targeting and systematically work through all those links and trying to acquire links back to your own site, it's time for a disciplined link-building program. The best way to manage your activity is by creating a spreadsheet like the one above that allows you to track and manage your activity. The previous image is a summary level but you should also create tabs on your spreadsheet that capture the sites you use for submission and additional techniques you use. This allows you to come back to authoritative sites on a monthly basis and reuse them for link submissions.

Your plan should be as follows:

1. Begin by developing an article or some type of original content for your website. Google thrives on original content, large websites, and authority. The best and fastest way to get there is with original content and an ever developing website. Begin your SEO campaign with a commitment to continually evolve your own website with new content. Make sure it is related to the theme of your website and grows steadily over time by adding two to five per month.

2. Do follow blog submissions. Each month, focus on making quality submissions to "do follow" blogs in your niche based on competitor backlink profiles. If you are unable to find do follow blogs in your niche, focus on high authority blogs of any kind. By taking the time to read posts and make value-added comments you can get the attention of the blog owner. When reaching out to blog owners to request a guest post to be genuine. Submit an article/post you've already written or a well thought through idea that is relevant for the blog audience. One way to improve your acceptance rate is to provide credentials or samples of your work. I also like to inform the blog owner that when he publishes my content I will share a link to the post via my large social network. Think about creating value and your chances of being accepted will grow exponentially.

3. Do follow blog comments. Leaving meaningful comments on do follow blogs, if implemented correctly, is a great source of authoritative links. I recommend no more than ten to twenty quality blog comments in a given month. Assuming you have a list of ten quality blogs, making a couple of comments on each should be easy. This also keeps things manageable. With most blogs there is moderation. As a result, your comments may take some time to appear live or may be rejected. Stay the course and you'll find more and more of your comments being accepted.

4. Forum submissions. As discussed previously forum submissions are a great resource for one-way links. On many forums you may need to make a minimum of ten posts before you are allowed to display your signature block including links back to your website. Register on a number of forums that you can go to on a monthly basis to post and display your signature. I suggest anywhere around twenty forum posts per month on average. The reason is that forum posting, much like blog posting, takes time to do correctly. If you're aggressive you could certainly use forum posting much more. I'd shoot for as much as fifty posts in a month if it's something you enjoy but it's not necessary. You may be asking why you would do so much with forums especially due to the fact that all you need is a single link from a forum to make it worthwhile. The reason is that social media now weighs very heavily into the success of forum marketing for optimization purposes. The more active you are, producing meaningful content, the more your posts will be shared – driving traffic and building authority to your profile and inbound links. This is definitely one of those tasks I'd consider outsourcing once you've established yourself on some targeted forums for your niche and have a means for producing quality content.

5. Profile submissions. Each month I use a freelancer to post on high-profile websites. Although Angela's packet offers around thirty potential links each month, invariably the list boils down to around twenty or so sites where you can easily place a one-way link back to your website. I use this list for all of the sites I'm optimizing and have even developed my own list of high-profile sites. If you are just starting out, try for about ten high authority profile submissions for your site each month. If more advanced and you have supplemented the sites provided on Angela's list, you can post up to twenty five over the course of a month. Once you've posted your link for a particular site on one of the suggested profile sites, do not post again until the following month. Duplicate links created at the same time won't help your link-building efforts.

6. Press Release Submission. Each month you should be distributing at least one press release per website. A release should be more than 350 words and have some type of "news". This could be something as simple as a new feature added to your website, a new customer, or a new service that you are launching. Then, make submissions to a few PR sites (e.g., Pr-inside, etc.). Once you have submitted to a press release distribution site, the news is distributed to hundreds of additional websites, news sites, and blogs. This is a great way to build quality links from many different sources. After each release is posted, share it on social media. This will increase the page authority of the page that carries the release which ultimately ties right back to your website.

7. Social Media Posts and Links. Social media is an important resource for communicating with others and posting links to your website and blog. Facebook, LinkedIn, Twitter, Google, Pinterest, and the like, are common social media sites that you should include your profile and be resources you post to on a regular basis. Include a link to your site in actual social media posts each month.

Develop an editorial calendar that focuses on topics related to your audience. Each week, generate 5 – 7 new posts that point to relevant information on your website or other high authority resources. As users see value in what you're sharing, they will share with others. Don't feel like all the content needs to be your own. Much of the content should reside on your site but it's unrealistic to always create the content. That's okay. As long as you are developing a following, providing value, and encouraging engagement, you're building your website authority. The links in your profile combined with additional links on your "Wall" and "Tweets" can build link equity that propels your search rankings. Encourage followers to redistribute your content whenever and wherever possible.

8. Video Submissions. I used to have video submissions and social media tied together for link-building purposes, and to a large extent, they are very much connected. YouTube is really one of today's largest social media sites and promoting video is necessary to gain full SEO benefit. Videos appear in search results and also carry authority that can be attributed to your websites. A good goal is to produce one to two new videos every month and post on video sites such as YouTube and Vimeo. Once posted, be sure to encourage views, ratings, and sharing via social media like Facebook and Twitter. Videos are commonplace and easy to distribute. Additionally, universal search results are picking up and displaying videos in search result listings. Always make sure to include a link to your site in the beginning of your video's description when submitting to video sites and use your keywords I the first 25 words of dialog. The most important thing is to be okay with self-created videos. People aren't looking for big scale video productions in high definition. Rather, create videos using your mobile device that cover an important topics for your audience. At the end of the day it's less about production quality and more about substance.

10. Local Search Engine Profiles. With the advent of local search comes dozens if not hundreds of websites designed for small businesses to list information about their company, products, and services. Seek out yellow page type listing sites and register for a free profile on each of them. Many of these sites ask for premier listing fees but a free listing is adequate in most cases. A number of these sites have become quite large and are a great place to acquire links. When completing your business profile, provide as much information as possible. Sites like *Citysearch* allow for 5 photos to be added to your account and provide additional features like connections to social media accounts. Name files with keywords and optimize the business profile. Seek out and add your site to as many as five business profile sites each month. Business profiles are a great way to expand your reach and acquire links from high authority websites. Again, consider using a data aggregator like Moz Local to properly optimize and distribute your information on a monthly basis. This can save you time and produce better results.

There you have it. This is the exact schedule, with minor tweaks from time to time, that I use on a monthly basis to optimize my own websites and blogs. I suggest that you spend the first few month of your SEO campaign working through each of the submission types on your own. Once you have a strong understanding and foundation for link-building strategies, find an outsource partner that can help with different aspects of the process. Before long, you'll be able to reduce the time spent with repetitive tasks and be able to focus on the next big search engine optimization project!

Conclusion

Increasing your ranking on Google and other search engines isn't complex, but it does take some time and effort. If you want to increase website rankings on a search engine results pages, begin by implementing the on-page optimization and the off-page optimization techniques you've learned in this book.

One question I seem to get quite often is, "How long does it take?" This is a difficult question to answer because it's relative. If you're trying to optimize for a keyword phrase like "eating blueberries on a Sunday afternoon," it will happen quickly, requiring simple on-page optimization and just a few articles with links back to your website using a proper link profile. On the other hand, if you are trying to optimize for a competitive term, and the top-ranked website has hundreds or thousands of incoming links, it can take a number of months to reach number one on Google. I can tell you from experience that more often than not, you'll put in a lot of effort and it will appear as nothing is happening or only small shifts are occurring. But stay focused and consistent. All of a sudden…wham! Your site will jump up in the search results unexpectedly. Stay the course and I guarantee you'll see results. Many fail because they give up too soon.

Regardless of where you're starting from, the key is persistence. These are the same techniques I've used to achieve top positions on Google for almost every keyword and keyword phrase that is important to my websites. Visualize your goal and take deliberate steps toward improving your search engine result placements daily and before long you will be exactly where you want to be— dominating the world's largest search engine.

To simplify your journey toward the number one position on Google, don't hesitate to use effective SEO tools and resources and continue learning about SEO. Although search tools, including outsourcing, aren't required for achieving top search engine placements, they can help you achieve your goal more quickly than manually implementing particular SEO techniques. Follow the strategies defined in this book; they've been proven effective time and again by many individuals who have already begun using these techniques. And don't hesitate to use all of the resources I've made available for those seeking top rankings at https://Bigfinseo.com/resources to advance your optimization program. I wish you the best of luck on your SEO journey. See you at the top and keep it simple!

A Final Request

Thank you for reading, *SEO Made Simple*, 7th Edition. If you feel this book has provided value, please visit Amazon.com and write a review.

I'm always looking for feedback (positive, negative, or neutral) and would love your comments on this book. I will provide you with access to my Ultimate SEO checklist (a $97 value) absolutely FREE! Simply send a link to your review once posted on Amazon.com to: mfleischner@bigfinsolutions.com

Connect with Us

Like our page on Facebook (Big Fin SEO) for updates and helpful SEO tips.

Section 4

SEO Glossary

Glossary

Below are some of the most common SEO-related words, phrases, and definitions. Some fellow authors who have reviewed my book in the past have said that I've wasted valuable space in these pages with an SEO glossary. I have to disagree. The glossary remains for the simple fact that I've heard from literally hundreds of individuals who appreciate the reference and use it on an ongoing basis.

Affiliate marketing - An online marketing strategy that involves revenue sharing between online advertisers and online publishers. Compensation is typically awarded based on performance measures such as sales, clicks, registrations, or a combination of factors.

AI – Artificial intelligence. Google is now using artificial intelligence and natural language programming to improve search results.

Alt tag - The alternative tag that the browser displays when the individual does not want to or cannot see the pictures present in a web page. Using alt tags containing keywords can improve the search engine ranking of the page for those keywords.

Alt text - Short for alternative text, it is used with an image and has a number of purposes. Primarily it is a placeholder for an image, so that if the image is slow to load or not shown, there will be an indicator of the content.

Anchor - Refers to a link on a web page, often found at the top or bottom of the page that allows users to move to specific content on the web page.

Anchor tag - Code determining the destination of a link.

Anchor text - The text part of any link, and of vital importance to any SEO effort. Instead of a link being displayed as www.marketingscoop.com, for example, using anchor text will allow the same link to be displayed as *Marketing Expert*. The search engines will then index the page based on this keyword.

Backlink - A link from one site that points to another. When getting backlinks, always ask the person linking to you to use anchor text.

Banner ad - A graphic Internet advertising tool. Users click on the graphic to be taken to another website or landing page. Banner ads are typically 468 pixels wide and 60 pixels tall, but the term can be used as a generic description of all online graphic ad formats.

BERT – Bidirectional Encoder Representations from Transformers is a technique for Natural Language Processing pre-training developed by Google.

Black hat - The use of unscrupulous methods to optimize a website. Discovery of these methods being used will often lead to a site being banned from major search engines.

Blog - A contraction of the term *weblog*, it is a form of Internet communication that combines a column, diary, and directory with links to additional resources.

Blogroll - A term used to describe a collection of links to other weblogs. Blogrolls are often found on the front-page sidebar of most weblogs. Various weblog authors have different criteria for including other weblogs on their blogrolls.

Browser - An individual searching the Internet for information. Also, a software package (Internet browser) used to view pages on the World Wide Web.

Caching - A computer process that stores web files to your computer for later access. These web pages are displayed without the need to re-download graphics and other elements of the previously visited page.

Canonical page - The preferred version of a set of pages with highly similar content.

Canonical tag – Html used to specify a canonical page to search engines. This is done by adding a <link> element with the attribute rel="canonical" to the <head> section of the non-canonical version of the page.

Cascading style sheets (CSS) - Used to manipulate and easily manage the design of a website.

Click - Each time a visitor clicks on a website or website link.

Click fraud - A form of theft perpetrated against advertisers who are paying per click for traffic, in which fraudsters may use automated means to click on your ads from spoofed IP addresses over random periods of time.

Click-through – A term used to measure the number of users who clicked on a specific Internet advertisement or link.

Click-through rate - The number of click-throughs per online ad impression, expressed as a percentage or exposure; a click on a link that leads to another website.

Click tracking - The use of scripts in order to track inbound and outbound links.

Cloaking - One of the most popular black hat methods, in which the visitor to the site is shown a page optimized to his search request, while the search engine spiders see a completely different set of pages designed to rank well.

Conversion rate - The percentage of targeted prospects that take a specified action within a given time frame.

Cookie - Computer code that is embedded in your Internet history file, allowing websites to recognize you as a returning visitor.

Cost-per-click - A specific type of cost-per-action program where advertisers pay each time a user clicks on an ad or a weblink.

Cost per thousand (CPM) - A simple and commonly used method of comparing the cost effectiveness of two or more alternative media vehicles. It is the cost of using the media vehicle to reach one thousand people or households.

Crawler - A program that goes through websites and gathers information for the crawler's creator.

Dead link - A link that produces a 404 error, page not found.

Deep linking - Connecting to a web page other than a site's homepage.

Deep submitting - Submitting all of your website's URLs—in other words, every page of your site—to a search engine. Most search engines forbid this practice.

De-listing/de-indexing - If search engines detect that you are using unscrupulous methods to get your site ranked, or if they regard your site as "spammy," they will remove your site from their index and it will no longer appear when users search for it.

Directory - A database of websites. Yahoo! and Open Directory are major examples. They are similar to search engines, except that the database is organized in a meaningful way by human beings. Many search engines use a directory as well as their own robots.

Domain name - The name assigned to a particular website (e.g., MarketingScoop.com).

Doorway page - A web page with content that's meaningful or visible only to the search engines; also called a *bridge page* or a *gateway page*.

Dynamic page - A page that generates content "on-the-fly" as a user requests the page.

eCommerce - An Internet-based business model that incorporates various elements of the marketing mix to drive users to a website for the purpose of purchasing a product or service.

Gateway page - A method once used to enable a site to rank well for a variety of keywords. It is frowned upon by the search engines and is no longer useful, as the search engines now base much of their algorithms on linking strategies.

Google - One of the most important spidering search engines by far, Google plays a dominant role in the search engine market.

Googlebot - The crawlers that index pages into Google.

Google Panda - A change to the Google's search results ranking algorithm that was first released in February 2011. The change aimed to lower the rank of "low-quality sites", and return higher-quality sites near the top of the search results.

Google Console – Google Search Console is a web service by Google which allows webmasters to check indexing status and optimize visibility of their websites.

Google My Business – A company profile available from Google allowing businesses to promote and engage with customers.

Google Penguin - A Google algorithm update that was first announced on April 24, 2012. The update was aimed at decreasing search engine rankings of websites that violate Google's Webmaster Guidelines by using black-hat SEO techniques, unnatural link profiles or anchor text, participating in link schemes, deliberate creation of duplicate content, and others.

Google Places – Previously referred to as Google Local. A search that produces local results based on proprietary google maps algorithm.

Google Plus - Was a multilingual social networking and identity service owned and operated by Google Inc. It was decommissioned in April 2019.

Google Preview – The ability see a website thumbnail image from the primary search page of a Google search result.

HTML – Stands for *hypertext markup language*. The coded format language used for creating hypertext documents on the World Wide Web and controlling how web pages appear.

HTML e-mail - An e-mail that is formatted using hypertext markup language, as opposed to plain text.

Header tag - An HTML tag that is commonly used for page headers.

Hidden text - Text that is invisible to the human eye because it is the same color as the background.

Hit - When a person visits a web page, that web page receives a number of *hits*—one hit for the page itself, and one for every graphic on the page. The number of hits is not regarded as an accurate measurement of a website's popularity.

Hit rate - Also considered the conversion rate, it is the percentage of the desired number of outcomes received by a person relative to the total activity level.

Homepage - The main page of a website.

Hummingbird Update – Google algorithm update integrating natural search language into their rankings calculation and further devaluing certain types of websites.

Impressions - The actual number of people who've seen a specific web page. Impressions are sometimes called *page views.*

Inbound link - A link from another website to your website.

Indexing - Behind-the-scenes creation of an ever-changing database based on the contents of web documents; search engines and filtering software use indexing to find and/or block documents containing certain words or phrases.

IP address - A unique number that identifies a computer or system.

ISP - Short for *Internet service provider*, an ISP is a company that provides access to the Internet.

JavaScript - A scripting language developed by Netscape and used to create interactive websites.

Keyword - A word that is entered into the search form or search "window" of an Internet search engine to search the web for pages or sites about or including the keyword related to it.

Keyword density - Keywords as a percentage of text words that can be indexed.

Keyword marketing - Placing a marketing message in front of users based on the keywords they're using to search.

Keyword stuffing - Placing excessive keywords into page copy and coding such as meta tags; this may hurt the usability of a page but is meant to boost the page's search engine ranking. Hiding keywords on a page by making them the same color as the page background and loading tags with repeated keyword phrases are examples.

Keyword weight - Refers to the number of keywords appearing in the page area divided by the total number of words appearing in that area. Weight also depends on whether the keyword is a single word or a multi-word phrase.

Lead generation - The process of collecting contact information and identifying potential sales leads.

Link checker - A tool used to check web pages for broken links.

Link farm - A series of websites linking to each other in order to increase rankings.

Link popularity - Often used as one of the criteria to determine rank on search engines, the measure of the quantity and quality of sites that link to your website.

Meta search engine - A search engine that displays results from multiple search engines.

Meta tags - HTML coding that is used to describe various features of a web page and appears in search result listings.

Navigation - Elements of a website that facilitate movement from one page to another.

Online marketing - A term referring to the Internet and e-mail-based aspects of a marketing campaign, which can incorporate banner ads, e-mail marketing, SEO, eCommerce, and other tools.

Open Directory Project (DMOZ) - A large directory of websites run by volunteers. Their database is used by many websites across the Internet.

Opt-in - A program where membership is restricted to users who specifically request to take part.

Opt-out - A program that assumes inclusion unless stated otherwise. The term also refers to the process of removing one's name from a program.

Optimization - Fine-tuning a website or web page with the ultimate goal being to ascertain a higher position in all or a specific search engine's results.

Organic listings - Listings that appear on a search engine solely because of merit, applicability, etc. In other words, listings that are not paid for; also called *natural listings*.

PageRank - Part of Google's search algorithm, it measures a page's popularity and is calculated in part by analyzing the number of links to a page from other sites and factoring in the importance of those pages. The highest rank is a score of 10 out of 10.

Page view - A request to load a single HTML page. Indicative of the number of times an ad was potentially seen or *gross impressions*. Page views may overstate ad impressions if users choose to turn off graphics (often done to speed browsing).

Paid inclusion - Paying to be included in a search engine or a directory index. May not improve search rankings but guarantees inclusion of pages a spider might have missed and "respidering" of pages periodically.

Pay-per-click - An online advertising payment model in which payment is based solely on qualifying click-throughs.

Pay-per-sale - An online advertising payment model in which payment is based solely based on qualifying sales.

Pop-under - An online advertisement that displays in a new browser window behind the current browser window and is seen when an individual closes his current browser window.

Pop-up - An online advertisement that displays in a new browser window without an overt action by the website user.

Public relations - The form of communication management that seeks to make use of publicity and other unpaid forms of promotion to influence feelings, opinions, or beliefs about the company, its products, or services.

Query - A search phrase submitted to search engines.

Ranking - The position of your website within the search engine indexes for a particular keyword.

RSS - Stands for *really simple syndication*. A lightweight XML format designed for sharing headlines and other web content. Typically, an RSS newsreader or aggregator is used to subscribe to syndicated RSS feeds.

Reciprocal links - An agreement where two website administrators agree to link to each other's websites.

Refresh tag - A tag that defines when and to where a page will refresh.

Robot - Any browser program that follows hypertext links and accesses web pages but is not directly under human control. Examples are the search engine spiders, the "harvesting" programs that extract data from web pages.

Robots.txt - If you wish to control which parts of your site a search engine spider indexes, you can use a robots.txt file to prevent the spider from indexing certain parts. Not all spiders will follow it, but it can be a useful tool if parts of your site are not ready for indexing.

SEO - Stands for *search engine optimization*. The process of developing a marketing and technical plan to ensure high rankings across multiple search engine results lists.

SERP - Stands for *search engine results placement*. Essentially, where your website is ranked on a given search engine for a chosen search term.

Search engine - A server or a collection of servers dedicated to indexing Internet web pages, storing the results, and returning lists of pages that match particular queries. The indexes are normally generated using spiders.

Search engine submission - The act of supplying a URL to a search engine in an attempt to make a search engine aware of a site or page.

Shopping cart - Software used to make a website's product catalog available for online ordering, allowing visitors to select, view, add/delete, and purchase merchandise.

Site search - A program providing search functionality across a single website or blog.

Skyscraper - A type of online ad that varies from a traditional banner size (468 x 60) and is significantly taller than the 120 x 240 vertical banner.

Social Media – Online resources developed for interaction among individuals using highly accessible and scalable publishing techniques. Social media uses web-based technologies to turn communication into interactive dialogues.

Spam - Unwanted, unsolicited e-mail, typically of a commercial nature.

Spider - A program that visits and downloads specific information from a web page.

Splash page - A branding page before the homepage of a website.

Stickiness - The amount of time spent at a website, often a measure of visitor loyalty.

Submission - Putting forward a site to a search engine or directory.

Thumbnail - A rough sketch or snapshot, usually of a website, that provides a small view of what a web page looks like in the form of a .jpg, .gif, or .png file.

Title tag - HTML code used to define the text in the top line of a web browser; also used by many search engines as the title of search listings.

Traffic - The visitors and page views on a website.

URL - Stands for *uniform resource locator;* an address that specifies the location of a file on the Internet.

Unique visitors - A measurement of website traffic that reflects the number of real individuals who have visited a website at least once in a fixed time frame.

Universal search - The integration of various media types into search result listings, including but not limited to websites, blogs, video, news, etc.

Viral marketing - A phenomenon that facilitates and encourages people to pass along a marketing message about a specific product, service, or company.

Web analytics - The process of using web metrics to extract useful business information.

Web browser - A software application that allows for the browsing of the World Wide Web.

Web design - The practice of selecting and coordinating available components to create the layout and structure of a web page.

Web directory - An organized, categorized listings of websites.

Web metrics - Statistics that measure different aspects of activity that transpire on a website.

Website - A site (location) on the World Wide Web. Each website contains a homepage, which is the first document users see when they enter the site. The site might also contain additional documents and files. Each site is owned and managed by an individual or company.

White hat - A reference to proper SEO methods that are approved by the search engines. Using these methods increases your chances of your site being permanently indexed in the search engines.

Whois - A utility that returns ownership information about second-level domains.

World Wide Web - A portion of the Internet that consists of a network of interlinked web pages.

XML feed - Simplified version of HTML that allows data (including product databases) to be sent to search engines in the format they request.

Additional questions or terms you need explained? Visit us online at https://bigfinseo.com to learn more.

Like our page on Facebook (Big Fin SEO) for updates and helpful SEO tips.

www.ingramcontent.com/pod-product-compliance
Lightning Source LLC
La Vergne TN
LVHW041213050326
832903LV00021B/601